Young Adult and Canonical Literature

Young Adult and Canonical Literature

Pairing and Teaching

Volume 2

Edited by
Paula Greathouse
Victor Malo-Juvera

ROWMAN & LITTLEFIELD
Lanham • *Boulder* • *New York* • *London*

Published by Rowman & Littlefield
An imprint of The Rowman & Littlefield Publishing Group, Inc.
4501 Forbes Boulevard, Suite 200, Lanham, Maryland 20706
www.rowman.com

6 Tinworth Street, London SE11 5AL, United Kingdom

British Library Cataloguing in Publication Information Available

Library of Congress Cataloging-in-Publication Data

Names: Greathouse, Paula, editor. | Malo-Juvera, Victor, editor.
Title: Young adult and canonical literature. Volume 1, Pairing and teaching
 / edited by Paula Greathouse, Victor Malo-Juvera.
Description: Lanham : Rowman & Littlefield, [2021] | Includes
 bibliographical references and index. | Summary: "The purpose of this
 collection is to offer secondary teachers engaging ideas and approaches
 for pairing young adult and canonical novels to provide unique
 examinations of topics that teaching either text in isolation could not
 afford"—Provided by publisher.
Identifiers: LCCN 2020046538 (print) | LCCN 2020046539 (ebook) | ISBN
 9781475860719 (cloth) | ISBN 9781475860726 (paperback) | ISBN
 9781475860733 (epub)
Subjects: LCSH: Young adult literature—Study and teaching (Secondary) |
 Canon (Literature)—Study and teaching (Secondary) | Youth—Books and
 reading.
Classification: LCC PN1008.8 .Y58 2021 (print) | LCC PN1008.8 (ebook) |
 DDC 809/.892830712—dc23
LC record available at https://lccn.loc.gov/2020046538
LC ebook record available at https://lccn.loc.gov/2020046539

Contents

Acknowledgments

We would like to thank our editor, Carlie Wall, for championing our project and getting us the greenlight to publish two volumes. Thank you, Carlie!!! We also want to thank all of our chapter authors who did most of their work during the early months of the COVID-19 pandemic, when schools were closing and, like most educators, they were suddenly thrust online to teach. We appreciate their dedication to students and to young adult literature.

Preface to Volume 2

When we had the idea for *Young Adult and Canonical Literature: Pairing and Teaching*, we had intended on curating a single collection of essays that would share new ways to combine young adult and canonical literature in secondary English language arts classrooms. We were excited about the project but had no idea we would receive so many unique and high-quality proposals. After reviewing them and discussing each one in depth, we concluded that we had many proposals that we were loath to reject but also realized we had too many for a single text. As such, we curated two volumes to offer educators a wide array of pairings and unique approaches.

Although organizing the volumes chronologically would be straightforward, we chose not to do so. Instead, we have separated our chapters so that each volume features a variety of time periods, topics, and pedagogical methods to make each effective as a stand-alone text. We hope you find the chapters as engaging and motivating as we do, and we hope you find success using the ideas presented in our collection with your students. Thus, without further ado, we are delighted to present *Young Adult and Canonical Literature: Pairing and Teaching, Volume 2*.

Introduction

Victor Malo-Juvera and Paula Greathouse

Whether it is competing for teaching time, for space in classroom and school libraries, or in debates about literary quality, it seems as though canonical literature and young adult literature are continually in conflict. Regardless of the tensions between them, it is apparent that for the foreseeable future, the canon will remain in classrooms as its texts are often required by circular mandates and often constitute the only narratives available in book rooms and anthologies. Similarly, young adult literature's popularity in classrooms has continued to grow as it is typically more relevant to students' lived experiences and to the conflicts they witness and endure.

The terms *canonical* and *young adult literature* may often be defined with slight variations, and although a thorough discussion of the characteristics and history of both is beyond the scope of this introduction, a brief examination of each will be of benefit. The canon we discuss is the one that is taught in middle schools and high schools around America, what Hill and Malo-Juvera (2018) defined as the *secondary canon*. Although the influence of literary critics and scholars often arises when considering canonicity, ultimately for a text to achieve *and* maintain canonicity, it must be taught (Bloom, 1994; Malo-Juvera & Hill, 2019). It should be of no surprise to secondary teachers that the latest national study found the following texts to be most frequently taught in grades 9 through 11 (starting with the most frequent): *Romeo and Juliet*, *To Kill a Mockingbird*, *The Crucible*, *Julius Caesar*, *Of Mice and Men*, *Night*, *The Great Gatsby*, *Lord of the Flies*, *Huckleberry Finn*, and *The Scarlet Letter* (Stotsky, Traffas, & Woodworth, 2010). The secondary canon's membership is definitely larger than the aforementioned titles, and for a complete overview of the secondary canon, see Hill and Malo-Juvera's (2018) introduction to *Critical Approaches to Teaching the High School Novel: Reinterpreting Canonical Literature*.

Young adult literature has also been assigned varying definitions, and our definition takes qualities from previous ones as we define it as literature that (1) is mainly "written for young people age eleven to eighteen" (Tomlinson & Lynch-Brown, 2010, p. 4), (2) is "marketed as 'young adult' by publisher(s)" (Tomlinson & Lynch-Brown, 2010, p. 4), (3) features a young adult protagonist (Small, 1992), and (4) features a main plot and conflict "related to and relatable to the lives of teenagers" (Malo-Juvera & Hill, 2019, p. 2; Small, 1992). We do not include what we would call crossover fiction such as *Lord of the Flies* and *Catcher in the Rye* as young adult literature and we concur with others (e.g., Malo-Juvera & Hill, 2019) who have identified *The Outsiders* as the seminal young adult novel. Regardless of definitions, there has been an explosion in the publication of young adult novels in the past two decades and they have become a cultural force, anchored by several series that have become blockbuster movie franchises such as *Harry Potter*, *The Hunger Games*, *Twilight*, and *Percy Jackson*.

Canonical and young adult literature are not mutually exclusive. A young adult novel can also be canonical; in fact, according to Malo-Juvera and Hill (2019), young adult titles such as *The Outsiders* by S. E. Hinton and *Speak* by Laurie Halse Anderson have already achieved canonicity as they are among the most frequently taught texts in a recent national survey of high school English language arts teachers (Stotsky, Traffas, & Woodworth, 2010). This comes as no surprise to most English language arts teachers as many have long advocated for combining the two genres in instruction. Joan Kaywell, past president of the Assembly on Literature for Adolescents of the National Council of Teachers of English, published a four-book series, *Adolescent Literature as a Complement to the Classics*, which was published from 1993 to 2000, and Kaywell followed that up with *Adolescent Literature as a Complement to the Classics: Addressing Critical Issues in Today's Classrooms* in 2010. Another pioneering text was *From Hinton to Hamlet: Building Bridges between Young Adult Literature and the Classics*, edited by Sarah Herz and Don Gallo (2005). All of the aforementioned texts shared ways for teachers to combine classic texts, such as *To Kill a Mockingbird*, *The Great Gatsby*, and *Romeo and Juliet*, with the young adult literature of their time, such as Robert Cormier's *Chocolate War* and Cynthia Voight's *The Runner*.

Although arguments of textual complexity and literary quality have periodically arisen in terms of comparing young adult and canonical literature, Miller and Slifkin (2010) rebutted those beliefs and argued for the inclusion of young adult literature in AP-level courses. Their position is echoed by the National Council of Teachers of English/Council for the Accreditation of Educator Preparation standards for teacher preparation which require that teacher candidates be knowledgeable with young adult literature (National Council of Teachers of English, 2018).

We concur and believe that one of the most important reasons for teaching young adult literature in English language arts classes is its relevance to students. We agree that canonical literature addresses timeless themes that are still important today, such as female sexuality and reproduction (*Scarlet Letter*), African Americans and the criminal justice system (*To Kill a Mockingbird*), capitalism and labor issues (*Of Mice and Men*), homosexuality and rape (*The Color Purple*), racism (*Othello*), and even the American dream (*The Great Gatsby*). However, because most canonical texts were written decades—if not centuries—in the past, they are often unable to address current social issues in ways that speak to contemporary adolescent readers. This is where we believe that young adult literature has the most to offer. Consider that recent young adult texts have tackled topics such as police violence (*The Hate U Give*), immigration issues (*American Street*), and the life of teens after gender reassignment surgery (*If I Was Your Girl*). Furthermore, young adult literature provides a more diverse array of authors and narrative voices that extend beyond the white male gaze that dominated the time period in which many canonical texts were written. Young adult texts have detailed rape from the victim's point of view (*Speak*), how children experience war (*Tree Girl*), and how queer teens handle religious issues when coming out (*The God Box*) and have chronicled racial issues with protagonists from almost every cultural group such as African Americans (*Monster*), Hispanics (*Mexican White Boy*), Asian Americans (*American Born Chinese*), and Native Americans (*Absolutely True Diary of a Part Time Indian*).

To a large extent, the recent changes in society and the wide array of young adult literature that address them have been a driving factor in our desire to create this collection that builds on and extends the work of pioneers in the field of young adult literature, such as Kaywell, Gallo, and Herz. In the last decade alone, the world has changed in seismic ways as marriage equality has been ruled on by the supreme court, social justice issues such as #MeToo and BlackLivesMatter have arisen, and issues of immigration and deportation have come to the forefront of political issues across the globe. Thus, there is a need for an updated text that shares strategies for combining canonical and young adult literature that reflects the changes society has experienced and continues to experience. Moreover, as young adult literature has grown into its own, there is a need for pairings that do not always center the canonical text.

THE COLLECTION—PURPOSE AND ORGANIZATION

The purpose of our collection is to offer secondary teachers engaging ideas and approaches for pairing young adult and canonical novels to provide unique examinations of topics that teaching either text in isolation could not afford. Our collection does not center canonical texts and most chapters show how both texts complement each other rather than the young adult text being only an extension of the canonical; in fact, some chapters even center the young adult text. The pairings offered allow for comparisons in some cases, for extensions in others, and for critique in all. Throughout this collection, authors use the term *secondary* as opposed to middle or high school, this is intentional as although many canonical texts are often associated with that level, we have known many teachers who have used texts such as *Lord of the Flies*, *Of Mice and Men*, *Catcher in the Rye*, among others, in both middle and junior high schools. We also refrain from specifying specific reading levels for any of the texts discussed, as we have found assigning Lexile and grade levels to be restrictive without adding any benefits. We intentionally leave those types of decisions to our teacher readers who know their students best. Similarly, although the pedagogical approaches offered within chapters align with current English language arts and literacy standards, we eschewed referencing any specific ones as lists of standards can become unwieldy in texts and because teachers can easily determine how activities meet their local requirements.

Each of the chapters is organized correspondingly, with an introductory section, a summary of texts, and then instructional activities for before, during, and after reading; furthermore, each chapter has extension activities that move beyond the texts. In many cases, activities build on each other, and in other cases, they exist independently, allowing teachers to pick and choose which fits their students best. Finally, we have ordered the chapters chronologically using the publication date of the canonical texts, though we want to reiterate that we do not intend this to center or privilege them over the young adult texts.

Our second volume opens with Chaucer's magnum opus, *The Canterbury Tales*, paired with the multi-authored young adult text *Feral Youth*. Shelly Shaffer's chapter focuses on the frame-narrative plot structure employed in each, where a narrator challenges other characters to tell stories as they complete a journey. Teaching strategies center on symbolism, characterization, and themes of the two texts, and the chapter also highlights multiple creative activities such as photography, art, picture books, knot-making, close reading, and review writing.

Feminist critical inquiry grounds Amber Spears and Ciara Pittman's chapter that pairs Charlotte Bronte's *Jane Eyre* with Marta Acosta's *Dark Companion*. Their chapter explores how second-wave feminist issues raised between the 1950s and 1980s, such as agency, oppression, gendered expectations, and patriarchy, influence the reading of each text. Engaging strategies such as the feminist critique circle, trading cards, and blackout poems are shared with aim of engaging students in feminist criticism while expanding literacy skills.

Michael Macaluso and Katie Macaluso pair Emily Bronte's *Wuthering Heights*, the second most frequently referenced text on the AP English literature exam, with Angie Thomas's award-winning and best-selling young adult novel *The Hate U Give*. Their chapter explores the influence, possibilities, and determinants of *setting* as a dynamic literary device, one that drives conflict, action, and consequences. In working within this social dimension of setting, complex identities of characters across these texts are highlighted to show how characters in each text must navigate and reconcile the rules of their respective settings in order to accept their complex identities. Through this focus and an explanation of related activities, readers will come to understand how they are forever negotiating their own distinct "settings" and identities.

Alcohol-fueled parties and tragedy drive Janine Darragh's chapter "'I Wish I Weren't so High': Substance Abuse and Addiction in *We Were Liars* and *The Great Gatsby*," which pairs F. Scott Fitzgerald's classic American novel with E. Lockhart's *New York Times* Bestseller in a contemporary look at addiction. Darragh's chapter examines displays of opulent wealth and characters who arguably struggle with substance abuse, addiction, and emotional wellness, as well as considering its impacts on individuals, families, communities, and the arts. Narration is also examined as the substance abuse and the secrets each narrator hides bring about questions of their reliability.

Richard Wright's story of Bigger Thomas's crimes in *Native Son* and Tiffany Jackson's complex first-person account of a Black teenager's murder conviction in *Allegedly* make for an engaging pairing in secondary English language arts classes: both novels feature protagonists of color who kill, do not have access to equitable educational opportunities, and face unfair and unjust judicial systems. In this chapter, Lisa Scherff provides strategies for addressing the nuanced events in both novels which bring issues of equity, truth, and boundaries to the forefront. This chapter also offers a timely critique of redlining and housing inequality as well as an important examination of the use of the *N*-word in literature and classrooms, whose importance extends far beyond these two texts.

Surveillance and privacy are featured in Sarah K. Burriss and Melanie Hundley's pairing of George Orwell's seminal dystopia *1984* with Cory Doctorow's *Little Brother*. Aspects of science fiction are discussed in depth, as well as comparison points that show how relevant each novel is to today's readers. Technological advances are analyzed in terms of their impacts on privacy and lessons also examine anti-technology narratives, as well as ideas for critiquing propaganda in each text. Many aspects of techno-totalitarian futures imagined in both texts are realized in much of our daily lives and this chapter provides activities related to intellectual freedom and social media that are especially relevant to contemporary students.

A pairing of powerhouse titles appears in this chapter by Katharine Covino, Anna Consalvo, and Natalie Chase, who combine William Golding's tale of stranded British school boys in *Lord of the Flies* with Robert Cormier's dark look at rebellion and punishment inside a Catholic boys school in his young adult novel *The Chocolate War*. Both novels are populated mainly by male characters and the settings of both highlight male-centric isolation, competition, and violence. The conflicts that arise in each story are results of cultures of hyper-masculinity, or, in current terms, "toxic masculinity." With this chapter's pairing, the authors offer teachers and their students the opportunity to think about both durable and malleable cultural imperatives around conceptions of masculinity from a perspective of gender theory and to critically consider culturally inscribed, gendered performances.

Our collection finishes with Crag Hill's pairing of two novels set during the Vietnam War, *Fallen Angels* by Walter Dean Myers and *The Things They Carried* by Tim O'Brien. Each is centered on their respective protagonist's combat experiences during a one-year tour of duty in Vietnam. For both, these experiences are difficult to process and both characters are worn down emotionally and wounded during battle. Hill's chapter provides teachers with curriculum to contextualize the war, to connect students with the soldiers depicted in the novels through letter writing exercises, and to enhance comprehension of the plot and characterization in the two novels.

REFERENCES

Bloom, H. (1994). *The western canon*. New York, NY: Riverhead Books.

Herz, S. K., & Gallo, D. R. (2005). *From Hinton to Hamlet: Building bridges between young adult literature and the classics*. Greenwood Publishing Group.

Hill, C., & Malo-Juvera, V. (2019). *Critical approaches to teaching the high school novel: Reinterpreting canonical literature*. New York, NY: Routledge.

Kaywell, J. F. (1993). *Adolescent literature as a complement to the classics*. Greenwood Publishing Group.

Kaywell, J. F. (2010). *Adolescent literature as a complement to the classics: Addressing critical issues in today's classrooms*. Lanham, MD: Rowman & Littlefield Publishers.

Malo-Juvera, V., & Hill, C. (Eds.). (2019). *Critical explorations of young adult literature: Identifying and critiquing the canon*. New York, NY: Routledge.

Miller, sj., & Slifkin, J. M. (2010). "Similar literary quality": Demystifying the AP English Literature and Composition open question. *The ALAN Review, 37*(2), 6–16.

National Council of Teachers of English. (2018). *NCTE/NCATE standards for initial preparation of teachers of secondary English language arts, grades 7-12.* Retrieved from https://ncte.org/app/uploads/2018/07/ApprovedStandards_11121 2.pdf.

Small, R. (1992). The literary value of the young adult novel. *Journal of Youth Services in Libraries*, Spring 1992, 277–85.

Stotsky, S., Traffas, J., & Woodworth, J. (2010). Literary study in grades 9, 10, and 11: A national survey. *Association of Literary Scholars, Critics, and Writers.* Retrieved from http://alscw.org/wp-content/uploads/2017/04/forum_4.pdf.

Tomlinson, C. M., & Lynch-Brown, C. (2010). *Essentials of young adult literature.* Boston, MA: Pearson.

Chapter 1

Feral Youth, The Canterbury Tales, and the Power of Stories

Shelly Shaffer

Marcel Proust (1934) once said, "We are not provided with wisdom, we must discover it for ourselves, after a journey through the wilderness which no one else can take for us, an effort which no one can spare us, for our wisdom is the point of view from which we come at last to regard the world" (p. 649). This cannot be truer than on the journey taken by 10 teens in the book *Feral Youth* (Hutchinson et al., 2017) and by the 29 pilgrims in Geoffrey Chaucer's classic *The Canterbury Tales* (Chaucer, 1400/1993).

Because excerpts from *The Canterbury Tales* are commonly taught in secondary English courses, pairing *The Canterbury Tales* with the young adult text *Feral Youth* helps to make the canonical text more accessible and relatable to students. Following the same story structure as Chaucer's *The Canterbury Tales*, *Feral Youth* was written as a frame narrative, with a narrator who challenges other travelers to tell stories along their journey. This chapter shares ways of teaching *Feral Youth* alongside *The Canterbury Tales*, including pairing this contemporary text with the classic text in engaging and unique ways. Because the plot structure of *Feral Youth* was inspired by *The Canterbury Tales*, this contemporary story may be able to bridge the experiences of modern youth with the experiences of pilgrims in medieval England. Additionally, Chaucer's stories "The Prologue," "The Knight's Tale," "The Miller's Tale," "The Pardoner's Tale," "The Wife of Bath's Tale," and "The Reeve's Tale" pair with tales included in *Feral Youth* in terms of theme and character motivation. Although there are other stories in *The Canterbury Tales* that could potentially pair with *Feral Youth* stories, I chose to include in this chapter stories that were commonly included in British literature anthologies, with the addition of "The Reeve's Tale."

The Canterbury Tales by Geoffrey Chaucer

The Canterbury Tales tells the story of a group of 30 travelers—29 pilgrims and 1 narrator—who are journeying to the religious shrine of the martyr, Saint Thomas Becket, in Canterbury. The journey begins at the Tabard Inn, located in Southwark, London, and the pilgrims' objective is to make a four-day pilgrimage to Canterbury, a distance of approximately 60 miles from London. In the story, the host is Harry Bailey, who suggests that as the group rides together to Canterbury, they entertain one another along the way by telling stories. Bailey will judge the stories and the best storyteller will win a meal at the Tabard Inn upon their return. Since the journey to Canterbury is long, the pilgrims are expected to tell two tales on the way to the shrine and two tales on the return trip; however, there are only a total of 24 tales included in Chaucer's collection and the book ends abruptly at the end of "The Parson's Tale," leaving readers with a somewhat unfinished journey. Within the 24 stories that are included, some are more memorable than others (i.e., "The Wife of Bath's Tale" and "The Knight's Tale") and readers quickly begin imagining themselves in Bailey's role: judging each story to determine the best one. The stories focus on life, mythology, and personal beliefs and ultimately reveal more about the storyteller than anything else. Before and after each story, Bailey shares commentary, along with reactions from other members of the traveling group, and this narration helps readers to transition into the next tale.

Feral Youth by Shaun David Hutchinson

In a modern-day refashioning of a frame narrative, *Feral Youth* tells the story of 10 young people who are part of an outdoor education program for troubled youth. The story's teens are dropped in the woods 18 miles from the camp with only their packs, which include "sleeping bags, empty canteens, little bottles of bleach to disinfect the water with, and the clothes on [their] backs" (p. 9). The young people in this group are not survivalists. They are kids, from diverse backgrounds, who have been sent to the camp in Zeppelin Bend, Wyoming, as a last chance to turn their lives around. Like Harry Bailey in *The Canterbury Tales*, Gio, the narrator of *Feral Youth*, challenges each of the other teens to tell a story as they journey through the woods and back to their camp. Gio announces the best story will win a prize of a 100 dollars, and he will be the judge. Throughout their 18-mile trek back to Zeppelin Bend, Gio shares commentary between each story, and members of the group often wonder if the storyteller is sharing the truth about their own lives or telling a made-up story.

BEFORE READING

Before reading these complex texts, teachers should build background information for students about the story structure and work to create interest among
students by sharing main ideas and themes (i.e., irony, friendship, trickery,
jealousy, women's rights, unintended consequences, power, and revenge)
presented in the texts. Although *The Canterbury Tales* are often introduced
by teaching students about Chaucer and medieval England, beginning this
unit by building background focused on the frame narrative structure since
this pairing was created based on the similar narrative style is encouraged.

Frame Narratives

To begin, the teacher should help students explore the structure of frame narratives; essentially the *story within a story* literary technique. This format is
an advanced writing strategy that involves authors choosing a specific narrative structure that contributes to the story's meaning and aesthetic; analysis
addresses reading standards that expect students to be able to analyze an
author's choices concerning story structure. Additionally, by analyzing this
narrative structure, writers will be able to apply sophisticated techniques to
their own narratives, addressing writing standards' expectations.

One way students can become familiar with this type of narrative structure
is to explore frame narratives. To introduce the concept, the teacher can present examples of simple frame narratives such as the picture book *Interrupting
Chicken* [Stein, 2016] or the opening scene from the movie *The Princess
Bride* [Sheinman & Reiner, 1987]. Each of these examples feature a point of
view that shifts from the main narrator to another story being told by another
character. This transports the audience to another story entirely. The time is
not always chronological when these shifts occur, nor is the setting consistent. These examples illustrate the shift in the story visually, so students can
see the transition between stories. This will make it much easier for teachers
to prepare students to identify these shifts in verbal narratives, such as *The
Canterbury Tales* and *Feral Youth*. After presenting the concept to students in
this easy-to-understand mode, the teacher can pose questions such as *Which
point(s) of view are being represented in the story? How does the author
transition from one story to the other?* or *Why do you think that frame narrative structure was chosen for this story?* These questions will help students
consider the reasons the writer chose to employ this story structure and help
students think critically about why they might use this structure in their own
stories.

Story within a Story—Photo Prompts

Using photos as prompts for students to create their own quick writes of stories within stories is one approach teachers can employ. Framing device photography, a common technique in photography, uses a *frame* within the picture to zero in on a particular aspect of the photo (Price, n.d.). By using a photo that features framing, students have an opportunity to consider the story behind as well as in front of the camera, thus being able to explore a story within a story (see figure 1.1 for a sample of a framed photo). Framing device photography includes photos where a picture is framed by natural frames (i.e., bushes, foliage, or blossoms); archways, tunnels, fences, doorways, or windows (wide open or partially closed); a door or frame in the background that frames the object in the foreground; hands or fingers that frame an object (as in the example); or any other objects that provide a frame to the picture being taken (i.e., rings, tubes, picture frames, magnifying glasses). After viewing a photo that uses framing device photography, students can write the story of what's happening in the photo and what's happening behind it, essentially creating their own frame narrative. This activity provides background information for students on the story structure used in *The Canterbury Tales* and *Feral Youth*, enabling them to enter the text(s) with knowledge of the complex features each contains.

Figure 1.1   Sample Framed Photo. Photo taken by Brandon Shaffer.

Exploration of Knots

To continue building background information before reading *The Canterbury Tales* or *Feral Youth*, students should consider the way the authors (Chaucer & Hutchinson) used symbols and words to imply meaning and push the audience to critically analyze characters' motives. Although several words and symbols could be taught with *Feral Youth* (i.e., truth, survival, feral), the most powerful symbol featured in the novel is the knot. *Feral Youth* includes several allusions to connectedness through the symbolism of knots throughout the novel. In particular, the Zeppelin Bend knot is used as a symbol in *Feral Youth*. The inclusion of the Zeppelin Bend knot adds depth to the readers' experience in the novel. This knot is often used in wilderness survival (Fontaine, 2005). The Zeppelin Bend knot got its name from its association with the airships, or dirigibles, in the 1920s called Zeppelins, in honor of Count Ferdinand von Zeppelin (Fontaine, 2005). These airships were enormous in size and had huge lifting capacity, which meant that the knots used to tie them down needed to be strong and able to take massive strain, yet be easily untied. The captains of the Zeppelin airships found that the best knot to fasten these huge airships was a knot that became known as the Zeppelin Bend (Fontaine, 2005).

The verbal irony of naming the camp in the novel *Zeppelin Bend*, after a famous knot, is apparent. The knot symbolizes how the 10 youth are connected through their mutual experiences. The narrator of the story, Gio, tells us in "Recipe for a Clusterfuck,"

> Zeppelin Bend isn't one of those summer camps where campers spend their time finger painting and canoeing and singing songs. It's the kind of place they send kids no one else wants and tell us it's our last chance to make a U-turn before we wind up in juvie until we're eighteen. (p. 5)

Part of the experience for campers at Zeppelin Bend was a wilderness survival trek, adding to the significance of the camp name—which symbolizes the traditional use of the Zeppelin Bend knot in survival training. Upon arriving at the camp, the 10 young people trained for three weeks on survival strategies prior to being dropped off in the middle of the woods at the start of the fourth week. The camp counselors told them they had three days to hike back to Zeppelin Bend, using their survival training and meager supplies to survive the journey. The teens did, in fact, make it back to the "Bend" in three days. During the three-day trek through the wilderness, a knot is formed between the campers as each share a story (or two), and the mutual experience connects the campers to one another. But within hours of returning to camp, Gio acknowledges that the campers probably won't remain friends after leaving the camp: "We might have tied ourselves to each other for the three days we spent in the woods, but those knots had already started to loosen now that we'd returned" (p. 306). The significance of the Zeppelin Bend knot is that it's strong, but it's also easily untied. This symbolism is clear in the relationships formed by the youth in the book.

The symbol of the knot not only implies the characters' interconnectedness, but the author includes a picture of a Zeppelin Bend knot illustration throughout the novel to show transitions between the stories in the frame narrative (see pp. 9, 24, 27, 64, 68, 105, 107, 121, 127, 149, 150, 187, 192, 209, 212, 226, 233, 265, 266, 287, 288, 302). This shows readers that the narrative voice is shifting and assists them in more easily following this shift. Readers could easily notice the symbol as a reading aid, but miss the significance of the symbol itself. The Zeppelin Bend knot is not mentioned at all in the text. The only way for readers to learn more about the knot and its importance as a symbol in the text is through additional research or background information.

To activate student interest in this symbol when introducing *Feral Youth*, I suggest providing twine or pieces of rope so students can create their own Zeppelin Bend knots. For step-by-step instructions, there are several videos online describing how to create a Zeppelin Bend knot, which would be a great way to grab students' attention to begin this activity prior to reading. For example, *Animated Knots* features an animation of how to tie a Zeppelin Bend in eight easy steps (Animated Knots, n.d.).

Students can also work in small teams to learn about various knots and their symbolism, particularly in relationship to how people choose to view knots in society. For example, knots symbolize binding in Chinese culture; the tying of a knot is said to be a symbol of good luck. Also, getting married is known as *tying the knot*. Students can work in small teams to research the symbolic meaning of knots in various cultures and religions. Some possible research topics could be Celts, Chinese, Egyptian, European, Japanese, Indian, Native American, Mexican, and Buddhist, among many others, or students could research the symbolic meaning of certain types of knots (i.e., bowline knot, clove hitch, alpine butterfly loop). Once teams complete their research, they can share and present their new knowledge to the whole class by creating a poster to share in a gallery walk. During the gallery walk, teams will share visuals of knots from the research, including how the knots are used in the culture or religion and what each knot symbolizes.

DURING READING

Because these texts are classified as frame narratives, they do not follow a typical plot structure; rather, the story within a story structure challenges readers to follow multiple plotlines at the same time. This is one of the reasons these texts can be demanding for students.

Tracking Character Traits and Plots

During the first, full reading of *Feral Youth*, students can complete a graphic organizer that tracks each of the characters' key traits as well as the plots of each story. This will help students address standards for reading literature, such as determining themes or central ideas in a text, providing summaries of a text, how characters are introduced and developed, and determining implied versus stated meanings in texts. (See figure 1.2 for a sample completed graphic organizer.)

Much of the information about each character is included in the prologue section, "Day 1: Recipe for a Clusterfuck," which contains Gio's descriptions of each of the other teens in the group (pp. 5–9). Students can use this information to create an initial list of character descriptors for each person. As students read the rest of the novel, tracking the various stories is valuable since there are several stories within the main narrative; documenting each character's story and the character traits revealed in the story they tell is important to analyzing the entire narrative. Students can reference this graphic organizer throughout the unit: for example, as they analyze stories in the post-reading activity, and as they create a frame technique illustration in the extension section.

Annotating Pairings

If students have not read through *The Canterbury Tales* prior to this activity, it is highly recommended that teachers take the time to do so. Because *The Canterbury Tales* not only employs a frame narrative story structure, it is also written in poetry, and some time will need to be dedicated to the first reading of the Canterbury stories. During students' first read through of an individual story from *The Canterbury Tales*, teachers will want to require close reading, in which students annotate the tale using the CHUQS (circle, highlight, underline, question, summarize) system (see figure 1.3), circling unknown words, highlighting key details, underlining important ideas about the plot, writing questions, and summarizing each page of text (Bailey, n.d.). Students should annotate in pairs so that discussion about the meaning of the text can occur while reading and annotating. This step will help the teacher to identify misconceptions and areas where students need additional help with comprehension of the text. By completing this activity during the first read-through, students will have a strong understanding of each story, which will help with the next activity, comparing stories from each text.

Characters	Stories
Jackie Armstrong: quiet, invisible, fan *of Space Howl*, interested in fan fiction	"Jackie's Story" (pp. 193-508) by Justina Ireland Starts off as a fan fiction story about *Space Howl*, a fictional science fiction television show. When the other travelers complain, she switches to tell a story modeled from *The Three Little Pigs*, which takes place in New Pork. The story told by Jackie includes irony, greed, and the inevitability of circumstance.
Tino Estevez: Mexican, quiet, angry beneath the surface, wants to be the group leader, biased toward rich people	"A Cautionary Tale" (pp. 151-186) by Stephanie Kuehn CJ receives a scholarship to go to an elite school in his home town. He is working as an escort one night to help people get back and forth from a beach party. As he escorts a kid named Hollis, he is drawn into a ghost story involving murder and mystery. With an ironic ending, the story focuses on revenge and righting wrongs.
Jaila Davis: short, attitude makes her seem bigger, cusses in three languages, Native American background	"The Subjunctive" (pp. 129-148) by Alaya Dawn Johnson Jaila and her siblings are in the desert, where her brother, the coyote, was murdered in a well. Jaila seems to be telling a mythical story that includes magic and animal spirits. The story includes facing your past—and your fears.
David Kim Park: obsessed with sex, convinced Big Foot or aliens are in the woods, asthma, YouTuber	"Big Brother, Part I" (pp. 108-120) and "Big Brother, Part II" (pp. 213-225) by E. C. Myers David's sister is having mysterious orgasms in her sleep. He tries to capture the mystery on video, but accidentally uploads the video to YouTube. The impact of the YouTube video devastates his sister, Alison, and she is now missing. David's story includes regret, greed, and jealousy, as well as right and wrong.
Jenna Cantor: rich, White, smart with math, quiet, not snobby	"Butterfly Effect" (pp. 11-23) and "Chaos Effect" (pp. 289-301) by Marieke Nijkamp After Jenna's grandpa moves in with her family, he starts molesting her. Nobody in her household, including her mom and dad, believes her when she tells them what's happening. Her parents think she's rebelling when her grades drop and she cuts and dyes her hair green. She eventually starts a fire to her grandpa's car and is sent to Zeppelin Bend as a result. The story shows how Jenna gained some power despite feeling powerless.
Lucinda Banks: angry, complains a lot	"A Violation of Rule 16" (pp. 267-286) by Suzanne Young There is a new dress code implemented at her high school, and Lucinda is targeted by one of her teachers. Eventually, she is more often out of class than she is in class, and the principal and the teacher come up with a solution of wearing a sweat suit with large words printed on it. Lucinda refuses to wear the clothes and decides that burning the clothes will be her way of protesting the dress code rule.
Sunday Taylor: acts like a good kid, meek exterior, Black, gay dads	"Self Portrait" (pp. 235-264) by Brandy Colbert Sunday goes to a new school in California. It is a school dedicated to arts and sciences, and she meets another Black kid named Micah. She starts becoming his friend and goes over to his house, where she meets his brother Eli. Eli tries to get her to turn on Micah by telling her Micah's a drug dealer. After that doesn't work, Eli frames Sunday by putting drugs in her school bag. When she's caught, she is sent to Zeppelin Bend camp.
Cody Hewitt: gay, loves old Hollywood movies, has knowledge of old movies and actors, doesn't belong, stole money, belongs to a religious family, in the closet with his family	"A Ruthless Dame" (pp. 28-63) by Tim Floreen Snubbed by the guy next door who he is interested in dating, Cody decides to take revenge after he discovers photos of nude boys and girls (including himself) on the guy's phone. He steals money and comes up with a master plan, inspired by film noire and femme fatales, to destroy the guy by showing the photos to his girlfriend.
Georgia Valentine: rich, White, girl, likes Beyoncé, has a gay best friend, type A, "never talks shit" (p. 8), hard worker	"Look Down" (pp. 69-104) by Robin Talley This is a ghost story about a summer camp attended by Georgia and her best-friend/turned worst enemy. The best friend and Georgia hear some strange sounds in the woods after telling ghost stories. The best friend/enemy falls down a ravine and dies after bullying Georgia for being afraid after hearing the ghost stories.

Figure 1.2 Sample Character and Plot Chart for Feral Youth. Created by author. *Note.* This figure includes the character from *Feral Youth* along with a description of that character's traits. There is also a summary of the stories, along with the young adult author of the story.

Analyzing Paired Stories

For the following text pairing activity, students will re-read chosen individual stories from *Feral Youth* and *The Canterbury Tales*. Teachers could choose

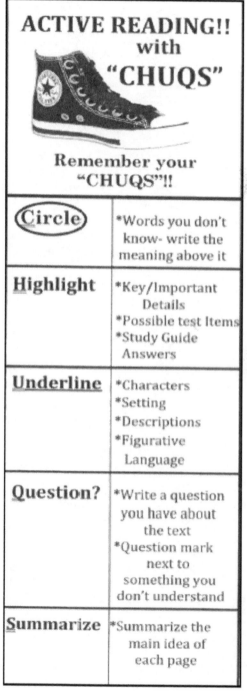

Figure 1.3 CHUQS Annotating System. Created by Kayla MacNeille.

one to two key pairings to analyze in depth or allow students to choose pairings; however, since time was already spent on understanding the frame narrative structure during the pre-reading activities, "The Prologue" and "Day 1: Recipe for a Clusterfuck" should not be analyzed in depth at this point.

In small teams, students can take turns reading the text aloud to one another while making note of themes, character traits, and big ideas presented in each story. This can be tracked in a graphic organizer that will enable students to make comparisons between the stories afterward. Through this close-reading comparison, students will make connections between the stories. This should help them see relevance in the classic story as it relates to themes and ideas that are still present in modern texts.

One example of a strong pairing is "The Reeve's Tale" (Chaucer, 1400/1993) and "A Ruthless Dame" (Hutchinson et al., 2017). Both of these stories address the theme of revenge, and in both stories, the characters carry out their revenge in a way that surprises the other characters. In "The Reeve's Tale," two students go to a miller with their grain. They are determined to fetch a good price and make a good deal without being cheated, but the miller steals and cheats them anyway. They trick the miller, convincing him to let them stay the night, and during the night, the boys play "musical beds," sneaking into bed with the miller's wife and daughter—ultimately infuriating the miller and leaving with their stolen grain. "A Ruthless Dame" shares Cody's story as he discovers he has been used by the guy next door and takes revenge after he discovers photos of nude boys and girls (including himself) on the guy's phone. He destroys the guy's relationship and reputation by showing the photos to his girlfriend. As students complete the comparison chart, they can identify the theme of revenge that is prevalent in both stories, and analyze whether the characters were justified in carrying out revenge. Students could also discuss with their teams the concept of revenge and what the authors of the story were trying to get readers to think about as a result of reading the story.

For the example comparison pairing, "The Reeve's Tale" (Chaucer, 1400/1993) and "A Ruthless Dame" (Hutchinson et al., 2017), characters in one text often share similar chrematistics to characters in the other text. Cody ("A Ruthless Dame") and the young scholars ("The Reeve's Tale") both feel taken advantage of. This is revealed through their actions and words (i.e., both exhibit naïveté during interactions with the stories' villains). The villains in the stories (Mike ["A Ruthless Dame"] and Haughty Simkin ["The Reeve's Tale]) also share characteristics which students could identify (i.e., taking advantage of others, tricking other characters into taking certain action, acting selfishly). There are also innocent victims (i.e., Simkin's wife and daughter and Mike's girlfriend) in both of the stories. These innocent characters become involved in the revenge, which ends up hurting not only the victims but also the innocents.

Finally, students can analyze the storyteller in each pairing ("The Reeve's Tale" [Chaucer, 1400/1993] and "A Ruthless Dame" [Hutchinson et al., 2017]). Students will want to consider each storyteller's (The Reeve and Cody) motivation for sharing the story, asking why do the Reeve and Cody tell this story? The stories are both entertaining, but were the characters motivated by different purposes than simple entertainment? This storyteller analysis will need to be clearly described to students since students are not analyzing Chaucer's or Floreen's motivation, but the motivation of the character in the text telling the story. The reactions of the other listeners in the text can also provide information about how the storyteller is perceived by his peers. Some of the characters laugh, while others don't believe the story is true, and some are angry (i.e., the miller in *Canterbury Tales* who feels personally insulted by the Reeve's story). Students can consider the purpose of the story, and decide whether they agree with the other character's reactions (i.e., Did the Reeve mean to make the Miller angry?).

Some additional pairings are offered in figure 1.4. These pairings address various themes and when choosing pairings to highlight, the teacher should use class interest(s) as a guide.

The Canterbury Tales	*Feral Youth*	**Shared Themes/Concepts**
The Prologue (pp. 1-23)	Day 1: Recipe for a Clusterfuck (pp. 5-9)	Sets up the challenge Introduces each traveler
The Knight's Tale (pp. 24-82)	Look Down (pp. 69-104) Jackie's story (pp. 193-208) The Subjunctive (pp. 129-148)	Irony Best friends falling out Retelling a familiar story Mythology
The Miller's Tale (pp. 83-102)	A Ruthless Dame (pp. 28-63)	Trickery Jealousy
The Pardoner's Tale (pp. 335-352)	Self Portrait (pp. 235-264) Big Brother, Part 1 (pp. 108-120) paired with Big Brother, part 2 (pp. 213-225)	Trickery Greed Unintended consequences
The Wife of Bath's Tale (pp. 176-186)	Violation of Rule 16 (pp. 267-286) Butterfly Effect (pp. 11-23) paired with Chaos Effect (pp.289-301)	Women's rights Power
The Reeve's Tale (pp. 103-115)	A Cautionary Tale (pp. 151-186) A Ruthless Dame (pp. 28-63)	Revenge

Figure 1.4 The *Canterbury Tales* and *Feral Youth*: Text Pairings. Created by author.

After students complete the comparison graphic organizer with their team, students can jigsaw into another team. For example, one person from team one moves to team two, three, four, and so on, so that each team is now a mixture of students from each team. In these jigsaw teams, students can compare their organizers and add details their team might have forgotten and share ideas other teams don't have on their charts. The teams should continue sharing until all of its members have had a chance to add to the organizer and all organizers throughout the room are very similar.

Next, the teacher can pose questions, hosting a whole class discussion once each team has completed their graphic organizers. Questions could be posed such as the following:

- What do we learn about the story's author through the story itself?
- What values are implied in the story?
- Which of the two stories did you prefer and why?
- In what ways are classic texts like *The Canterbury Tales* still relevant in the 21st century, if at all?

All of these questions ask students to use higher-order thinking skills, asking for textual evidence and examples to back up their opinions. This will push students to further engage with analysis of the stories and use critical thinking skills.

Following this close-reading analysis and discussion, the teacher can ask students to write a response to one of the discussion questions, using the evidence. And, through all of these during reading activities, students will be able to engage with both texts, *Feral Youth* and *The Canterbury Tales*, in important ways that will push their thinking and work to develop their reading skills.

AFTER READING

After reading sophisticated texts like *The Canterbury Tales* and *Feral Youth*, students should engage in discussion activities as well as a culminating activity that connects the main ideas from the pairing. A common after-reading activity is to write a frame narrative that models the narrative structure of these stories. This is a great way to use these texts as models; however, a literary analysis essay would better fit the standards and expectations.

Writing a Review

After reading the texts, students will soon realize that both Harry Bailey and Gio avoid crowning a winner to the story contest. Since the premise for the *main story* in each of these collections is to earn a prize, readers are left to wonder if a winner was ever determined and may wish to decide a winner for themselves.

For this after-reading activity, students write a critical review of one of the stories in either *The Canterbury Tales* or *Feral Youth*, in which they provide a rating for the story along with a written review. Students often see this type of writing in their everyday lives (i.e., film and television reviews on Rotten Tomatoes, product and book reviews on Amazon, and book reviews on Goodreads, BookTube, etc.), and because writing reviews is common in online environments, it is useful to model and teach this type of writing in the classroom.

Teachers can introduce this assignment by sharing a video book review from an established BookTuber (i.e., Little Book Owl, Life is a Page Turner, Thoughts on Tomes). Students can watch the video book review and take notes on specific components the BookTuber includes in the review. Questions to ask students to consider while watching the video include the following: *How is the book introduced? How much detail does the reviewer provide about the book? How does the reviewer share his/her/their opinion about the book? What other information about the book is shared in the video?* Students can share their findings with partners after the video, and the class can create a list of strategies the BookTuber included in the review that can be revisited as students consider the characteristics of written reviews.

Since this review assignment is a written review of the book, the teacher should follow the video book review with written models of effective reviews for students to read and analyze together. There are many sites online where teachers can find effectively written reviews to use as models for review writing. For example, *Kirkus Reviews* provides a strong model for writing a reviews, although stories are not starred/rated. Other sources for excellent models include *BookList, The School Library Journal*, and *Publishers Weekly*. To find non-examples, teachers could search for reviews on *Goodreads*, where amateur book reviewers can post their opinions and provide ratings on books. As students read and analyze examples and non-examples of book reviews, the class can add to and revise the list of strategies used by reviewers, which was begun with the BookTube video analysis.

For this assignment, students' reviews should follow an established review format. The teacher should require that the review includes evidence relating to character development, story format, theme, relatability, and other key factors that are expectations for effectively reading and analyzing literature. It is likely that students have discovered many of these characteristics on their own through analysis of the models provided by the teacher. But a formal review format by Jaigirdar (2019) suggested six steps for successful book reviews, which can be adapted to fit for the short stories being analyzed in this assignment. These steps include the following:

- Begin with a brief summary.
- Pick out the most important aspects.
- Include brief quotes as examples.
- Write a conclusion that summarizes everything.
- Compare to similar stories.
- Give it a star rating.

Beginning with a summary helps to provide context for the reader prior to diving into the more complex analysis that will be presented in the review. Next, students should analyze important aspects of the story, including characters, world-building, themes, and plot. Students should use textual evidence to support their analysis by including quotes to illustrate important parts of the story. Since some analysis has been done in the "comparing stories" assignment presented earlier in this chapter, if students have already analyzed two or more stories by comparing *The Canterbury Tales* and *Feral Youth*, some valuable information from their comparison chart can be used in the review if they choose one of those same stories.

Following the writing of the story review, teachers can ask students to work in small teams to peer review one another's writing. Based on Jaigirdar's (2019) tips for writing effective reviews, the following questions can be used to guide students:

- How did the writer introduce the book? Does it grab the readers' attention right from the start? What could the writer do to make the hook more effective?
- Did the writer include an effective summary of the book? What characteristics of the summary are strong, and which need improvement?
- How does the writer share important aspects of the book? For example, is the central idea or theme of the text included? How are characters developed throughout the text? What is the setting of the story and how does it contribute to the story? Is there anything missing?
- Does the writer back up the analysis with examples from the text/quotes? Does the analysis illustrate why the author likes or dislikes the story? Are there clear reasons written in the review that back up the author's opinion about the story?
- What makes it better or worse than other stories in the collection? Does it compare to any other books or stories you've read? Does this make the story stand out above the others?
- How does the writer wrap up the review? Does it leave the audience hanging at the end or is the conclusion satisfying? Does it avoid spoilers?
- What rating does the writer provide? Does this story deserve to win the prize over the other stories in the collection?

After students write their reviews, they can present their review by posting a video (on YouTube/BookTube), by posting their written review on a bulletin board in the classroom, or by posting their review online (Amazon, Goodreads).

EXTENSION ACTIVITIES

Creating a Visual Frame

To bring the unit full circle, teachers could have students create a frame technique illustration to represent the narrative structure and various stories within the text. This visual frame illustration should include space along the outside of the frame to depict keywords and events from the main story, and then on the inside of the frame, students will share keywords and events from the stories within the main story (see figure 1.5). This visual depiction of the frame narrative structure used in both *Feral Youth* and *The Canterbury Tales* will help students better understand and analyze the structure employed by

Figure 1.5   Visual Frame Example. Created by author.

Title	Summary
Gaiman, N. (1994). *The Sandman vol. 8: World's end*. NY, NY: DC Comics.	In the eighth volume of Neil Gaiman's *The Sandman*, the story entitled "World's End" features a group of travelers trapped at an inn between worlds, going around a table telling stories. "World's End" is also modeled after *The Canterbury Tales*
Gidwitz, A. (2016). *The inquisitor's tale: Or, the three magical children and their holy dog*. NY, NY: Dutton Children's Books.	In the year 1242, travelers from across France meet at an inn and begin to tell stories of three children. The children's adventures take them across France, where they encounter multiple dangers that push them to the brink of disaster on several occasions. This book has been compared to *The Canterbury Tales* since the central story is told by multiple storytellers.
Hamilton, P. F. (2018). *Salvation*. NY, NY: Del Rey	In this space thriller, a new technology has rendered many forms of transportation obsolete. But, when a crashed alien ship is found on a planet 89 light years from earth, 17 human lives are impacted. The interweaving storylines in this novel reveal how humanity ended up at this moment and also contemplates the future consequences.
Simmons, D. (1989). *Hyperion*. NY, NY: Bantam Books.	In this novel, Simmons creates a world called Hyperion, which exists beyond the law of the Hegemony of Man. A creature called the Shrike is worshiped and feared by those who live on this world. As Armageddon approaches, seven pilgrims voyages to Hyperion to find answers.
Zarins, K. (2016). *Sometimes we tell the truth*. NY, NY: Simon Pulse.	Zarins' (2016) *Sometimes We Tell the Truth* is a modern retelling of *The Canterbury Tales*. As a group of teens take a bus ride to Washington D.C., each tells a story in pursuit of the ultimate prize: a perfect score.

Figure 1.6 **Additional Young Adult Frame Narrative Novels.** Created by author.

Hutchinson et al. and Chaucer. Additionally, students will be able to recognize this structure in other texts and media they encounter.

Outside Texts and Film

The teacher could also choose to use this visual frame on an outside text or film. In that case, students would analyze the text using their newly acquired knowledge of frame narrative structure. The teacher could provide a list of complementary texts that could be used for this extension activity. There are several young adult novels, as well as movies, television shows, and other texts that follow the frame narrative story structure, teachers could provide a list of these for students to choose from. Figure 1.6 offers some suggested young adult frame narrative novels that can be paired with *The Canterbury Tales*.

CONCLUSION

Through the activities presented in this chapter, teachers can build student interest in a classic story by pairing it with a young adult text that relates to modern lives. *The Canterbury Tales* has continued to be included in ELA curriculum because its stories include timeless elements that make it relevant, even when read hundreds of years after the pilgrims first journeyed to Canterbury.

While creating an opportunity for students to learn about a common story structure, the frame narrative, this unit focuses on developing reading and writing skills that students will encounter and be able to use beyond school. The unit also provides an opportunity for students to polish their critical reading, comparing and contrasting, literary analysis writing, and many other skills that are deemed important in school.

REFERENCES

Allen, J. (2009). *McDougal Littell literature: British literature.* Evanston, IL: McDougal Littell.

Animated Knots. (n.d.). Zeppelin bend. *Animated Knots.* https://www.animatedknots.com/zeppelin-bend-knot.

Bailey, K. (n.d.). *Chuqs annotation system.* Arizona State University: unpublished work.

Beers, K., Jago, C., Appleman, D., Christenbury, L., Kajder, S., Rief, L., & Holt, Rinehart, & Winston, Inc. (2009). *Elements of literature: 6th course.* Austin, TX: Holt, Rinehart, and Winston.

Chaucer, G. (1993). *The Canterbury Tales* (R. L. Ecker & E. J. Cook, Trans.). Palatka, FL: Hodge & Braddock, Publishers. (Original work published 1400).

Fontaine, R. (2005, May 3). How to make a Zeppelin bend knot. *Survivaltopics.com.* http://survivaltopics.com/how-to-make-a-zeppelin-bend-knot/.

Hutchinson, S. D., Young, S., Nijkamp, M., Talley, R., Kuehn, S., Myers, E. C., Floreen, T., . . . Colbert, B. (2017). *Feral youth.* New York, NY: Simon Pulse.

Jaigirdar, A. (2019, February 14). How to write a book review: 6 steps to take. *Book Riot.* https://bookriot.com/how-to-write-a-book-review/.

Price, N. (n.d.). Photography composition–Framing. *Photography Vox.* http://www.photographyvox.com/a/photography-composition-framing/.

Proust, M. (1934). *Remembrance of things past* (Vol. 1, C. K. Scott Moncrieff, Trans.). New York, NY: Random House. (Original work published 1925).

Shaffer, B. (2020, April 15). [Untitled photograph of sample framed photo].

Sheinman, A., Reiner, R. (Producer), & Reiner, R. (Director). (1987). *The princess bride* [Motion picture]. United States: Twentieth Century Fox.

Stein, D. E. (2016). *Interrupting chicken.* Somerville, MA: Candlewick Press.

Wiggins, G. P., Pearson Education, Inc., & Prentice-Hall, Inc. (2012). *Prentice Hall literature: The British tradition: Grade 12.* Upper Saddle River, NJ: Pearson/Prentice Hall.

Chapter 2

Exploring Feminist Themes in *Jane Eyre* and *Dark Companion*

Amber Spears and Ciara Pittman

Reading *Dark Companion* in tandem with *Jane Eyre* offers students opportunities to explore author positionality while comparing and contrasting feminist themes. In particular, this pairing allows students the opportunity for in-depth exploration of the challenge to dominant patriarchal society in an effort to overturn traditional expectations of behavior. There are three main waves of feminism. This chapter explores second-wave feminist issues raised between the 1950s and the 1980s. Issues addressed in second-wave feminism include gender equality and discrimination, challenging women's roles in the home, workplace, and in politics.

Traditionally, feminist theory challenges knowledge about gender and critically explores oppressed groups in comparison to dominant groups. In this chapter, we explore how agency, oppression, gendered expectations, and patriarchy countertradition. As students work through the texts, they will have opportunities to study, analyze, and compare main characters in *Jane Eyre* and *Dark Companion* through a feminist lens. In doing so, it allows students to negotiate ways of knowing and doing from multiple perspectives as they learn about how gender works in the world (Hesse-Biber, 2012). As students increase their critical awareness of feminist ideologies, they might begin asking how gender, race, and class influence the narrative being told.

Jane Eyre by Charlotte Bronte

Young orphan Jane Eyre is sent to live with her aunt who is cruel and unkind. Jane is later sent to Lowood School, where the harsh living conditions continue for eight more years. Jane applies for and is hired as a governess for a wealthy man, Mr. Rochester. They fall in love and plan to be married, but Jane finds out on her wedding day that Mr. Rochester is already married to another woman whom he has been hiding in his home all along. Heartbroken, Jane leaves the Rochester estate in pursuit of a new life. She begins teaching, meets a clergyman named St. John (who turns out to be her cousin), and receives a substantial fortune left to her by her late uncle. Admitting her continued love for Mr. Rochester, Jane declines St. John's marriage proposal. She travels back to Thornton, discovers Mr. Rochester has been burned in a fire, and learns that his wife has passed away. Jane's love for Mr. Rochester prevails, and they are soon married.

This classic illustrates themes involving classism, oppression, gendered expectations, agency, and patriarchy. Jane's early life is fraught with difficulty as she deals with discrimination due to her familial disconnect, poverty, and gender. Despite these adversities, she grows up to become governess in Mr. Rochester's home. All along she demonstrates through her thoughts, words, and actions that she does not want to become Mr. Rochester's possession. Jane experiences much conflict throughout the story and struggles to maintain her agency. How will she navigate her expected duty as a lower-class citizen against the passion she feels for Mr. Rochester? How can she remain true to herself when adhering to societal expectations? We learn that Jane is the only one who knows what is best for her as she pursues her passions and never gives up on her dreams.

Dark Companion by Marta Acosta

Like Jane Eyre, Jane Williams was orphaned in her early childhood. Lacking resources, family, and stability, Jane spent her youth in foster care feeling unlovable. In a violent, gang-controlled neighborhood, Jane lacked the opportunity, social support, and a rigorous learning environment. Regardless of gender, poverty, and lack of opportunity, Jane asserts her agency and overcomes adversity. As a result, she was selected to receive a full scholarship to the prestigious Birch Academy. While at Birch Academy, the headmistress, Mrs. Radcliffe, showers Jane with special treatment: a customized school schedule, a home to herself, a clothing allowance, and a fully stocked pantry. Although new to the school, Jane easily becomes friends with a group of girls who are powerful, have money, and exude privilege. Akin to Jane Eyre, Jane Williams develops romantic feelings for someone outside her social class. Consequently, she is expected to parallel the lives of the Birch Grove elite in her dress, speech, and social calendar, forfeiting her autonomy for the economic and social security she had never had before.

Despite having access to things she never before dreamed, Jane soon feels unrest as she realizes things are amiss. She is excited by her new privilege, but cannot silence the questions she has about the movement in the woods, a death at Birch Grove Academy, and the sudden disappearance of the scholarship winner before her. As an intelligent and independent teen, she must determine who she is and what she wants from life. Ultimately, she regains her autonomy, pieces together the puzzle, and saves Birch Grove Academy from destruction.

BEFORE READING

Vampires

Both Jane Eyre and *Dark Companion* use gothic elements and suspense to capture readers' attention and establish plot. As a contemporary retelling, *Dark Companion* extends the gothic, supernatural elements in *Jane Eyre* to include vampires. Teachers can take advantage of these intriguing elements to engage readers, introduce the unit, and practice examining texts, by critically viewing clips from grade-appropriate vampire film trailers such as *Cirque du Freak: The Vampire's Assistant, Buffy the Vampire Slayer*, or a compilation of vampire films such as *Vampires in Film/TV* (DigitalGuru101, 2020a). Because this unit asks students to evaluate the depiction of female characters, teachers can also use these clips to practice by comparing the depiction of vampires in each. This approach should spark interest while introducing critique before delving deeper into the texts through a feminist lens.

Before watching the film clips, ask students to draw a picture of a vampire. No other instructions should be given. After about five minutes, have students share their pictures and discuss why they illustrated the vampire as they did. Next, teachers can explain that just as students made decisions in the role of illustrators, directors and authors make decisions in their depiction of characters as well. To apply this, students will evaluate the directors' representations of vampires. To help with examination, pose these critical questions: *How do directors represent vampires differently (looks, actions, speech, etc.)? How does your view of vampires change as a result of how the director depicts the vampire? How do the directors' depictions challenge your ideas of who/what vampires are? Why might the director have chosen to represent the vampire in this way?* After sharing their answers, students should watch the clips again, making notes of the directors' decisions. Alternatively, teachers may view film trailers from any two renditions of Jane Eyre looking at the representation of the protagonist before reading begins. This activity would also launch the text and provide practice with evaluation skills students will use in later study of the texts.

Feminism and Literary Critique

Although secondary standards often ask students to analyze and evaluate texts, literary criticism, a form of analysis, is largely absent from secondary studies. Looking at the texts through various critical lenses allows students to analyze for specific purposes, see different perspectives, and engage in critical literacy. The teacher should begin by introducing feminism and literary critique. Figure 2.1 provides a list of definitions of feminism that students should come to know. Ask students to discuss the definitions, thinking about what is and is not represented in each.

Next, teachers should model feminist criticism by critiquing short video clips from various current television shows, movies or use a compilation video such as *Women in Film* (DigitalGuru101, 2020b). By providing a list of questions that help students think through the text (the video clips in this instance), the teacher can illustrate how the questions frame one's understanding of gendered themes. Some guiding questions include the following: *How do women conform to or redefine stereotypical gender expectations in this piece? How do women illustrate or exemplify feminist themes in this piece? How does the text exemplify or contradict your understanding of feminism?* As students work through these questions, have them consider the following:

- Who is speaking?
- Who is silenced?
- What's missing in this story?

Sources	Definitions
Feminism. (n.d.)	The doctrine advocating social, political, and all other rights of women should be equal to those of men.
Grbich, C. (2013). p. 69	There is inequality in our society which has been constructed along gender lines and this has left women as a group subordinated to men in terms of socioeconomic status and decision-making power; structural and cultural expectations and practices continue to reinforce these inequalities.
Kelly, (2017).	The advocacy of women's rights based on the equality of the sexes. The feminist maxim: the personal is political.

Figure 2.1   Definitions of Feminism. Created by authors.

- How do race, gender, class, and sexual identities of characters or persons affect the trajectory of the narrative?
- How might your understanding of the text have changed if the ideas of race, gender, class, and sexual identities of characters had been different?
- Why did the director/producer choose to portray women in stereotypical or non-conformist ways?

	Women in Film Compilation Video Response Sheet	
Question	**Response**	**Theme**
Who is speaking?	In *Zombieland: Double Tap,* Madison (the blonde woman) is speaking, but she is depicted as unintelligent, representing the dumb, white blonde girl stereotype. In *Beauty and the Beast,* Gaston represents a dominant male stereotype and is speaking over Belle, pressuring her to accept his proposal.	Gendered expectations Patriarchy
Who is silenced?	In *Beauty and the Beast,* Belle is speaking, but she is not heard by Gaston. He continues to pursue her despite her lack of interest. He expects her to be interested in fulfilling a relationship role for him regardless of her wants or feelings.	Gendered expectations Patriarchy
What's missing in this story line?	In *Stranger Things,* Max shows El women's expectations of women by teaching her how to be herself. Who/what helped the women like Belle and Nakia develop agency?	Agency
How do race, gender, class, and sexual identities of characters or persons affect the narrative?	In *Black Panther,* Nakia is prepared to fight and becomes the heroine in the scene. I don't usually see this in the movies I watch on TV. The men are always the fighters and protectors.	Agency Gendered expectations
How might your understanding of the text have changed if the characters had been different?	In the clip from *Stranger Things,* El's friend Max takes her shopping and reminds her that it doesn't matter what Hopper or Mike thinks she should wear or look like. It was awesome to see El embrace who she was and what she wanted to wear as she stayed true to herself rather than conforming to others' expectations.	Oppression Agency Gendered expectations
Why did the director/producer choose to portray women in these stereotypical or non-conforming ways?	In *Zombieland Double Tap,* Madison is intended as a comedic figure and maybe for sex appeal. She serves as a relationship interest. *Beauty and the Beast* was produced a long time ago. I wonder if producers were even thinking about alternative ways to represent male and female characters? A lot of movies are created so that the woman is rescued by the man.	Agency Gendered expectations

Figure 2.2   Sample Completed Feminist Criticism Question Guide. Created by authors.

Students should record their answers to the guiding questions in a graphic organizer (see figure 2.2 for example). Once completed, open a discussion allowing students to share what they recorded and discuss how their understandings of feminism have changed since exploring film clips. For example, after viewing *Women in film*, students may explain how they thought oppression was something physical, but now understand that El was oppressed by the men in her life and unable to use her clothing as an outlet for her personality until Max helped her exert agency. Students may reference the Grbich (2013) definition and explain how they saw this definition in action when oppression happened in a common, everyday experience. Students might express how their thoughts of feminism have changed in relation to other components such as representation. For instance, students might say they now understand how representation of women in films can influence how women are viewed in life or how young women believe they should behave.

Next, the teacher could model feminist criticism through the poem that opens *Dark Companion*, "Paper Matches" by Paulette Jiles (1973). Provide students a copy of the text along with annotation materials: sticky notes and highlighters (yellow, blue, pink, green). Students begin by reading the poem in its entirety. Ask students to read the poem again, annotating the areas of the poem that correspond with areas of feminist critique based on the abstract nouns, or thematic topics, of feminist criticism (see table 2.2). Next, have students discuss their reactions to the text: *Which colors were used most in your highlighting? Were there any colors you didn't use? What messages did this convey about the poem you read?* Students could use their highlighted notes to discuss how the poem exhibits thematic feminist ideals. Finally, students could answer the two essential questions: *How do women conform to or redefine stereotypical gender expectations in this piece? How do women illustrate or exemplify feminist themes in this piece?* At this point, have students sketch an image that represents feminism. Later, as students acquire knowledge and examples that support their understanding of the themes from the texts, they will be able to describe, in words, their evolving understanding of feminism. This guided practice will serve as a launchpad to introduce students to feminist thematic topics and prepare them to examine the novels later in the unit.

Since students are breaking down the text and critiquing how it supports or refutes particular feminist themes, these types of activities will frame students' understanding of feminism and literary criticism as they walk through the process with a shorter text. Furthermore, this activity will ensure students' understanding of the concepts that will help facilitate discussion in the anchor texts by providing students with applicable definitions and

Topics	Definition	Possible Textual Examples
Oppression	Systematic patterns of power and control perpetuated against women and girls due to gender or class	*Jane Eyre*, Chapter 4, page 30 *Jane Eyre*, Chapter 12, page 115 *Jane Eyre*, Chapter 23, page 271 *Dark Companion*, page 202–205
Agency	The capacity of individuals to make their own decisions and act freely outside of influences such as gender	*Jane Eyre*, Chapter 23, page 272 *Jane Eyre*, Chapter 28, 350–351 *Jane Eyre*, Chapter 34, 432–433 *Dark Companion*, page 205 *Dark Companion*, page 226
Gendered Expectations	Behaviors, values, and attitudes that a society considers appropriate for a gender	*Jane Eyre*, Chapter 12, page 113 *Jane Eyre*, Chapter 35, page 452 *Jane Eyre*, Chapter 23, page 271–272 *Dark Companion, page 123* *Dark Companion,* page 156
Patriarchy	The conceptualization of how men and masculinity are seen as better than, more respected than, and hold more privileges than women.	*Jane Eyre*, Chapter 34, page 444 *Jane Eyre*, Chapter 28, Page 353 *Jane Eyre*, Chapter 16, page 170 *Dark Companion,* page 266

Figure 2.3   Thematic Topics of Feminist Criticism. Created by authors.

categorization schema for study of the novels during and after reading. (See figure 2.3).

DURING READING

Students often struggle with the dense and archaic language of canonical texts, but reading *Jane Eyre* and *Dark Companion* in tandem engages students with thematically similar texts and provides an opportunity for comparison. We suggest reading the novels using the schedule in figure 2.4. We have only included the main events from *Jane Eyre* to streamline your comparison study. Feel free to exercise agency in determining your own reading schedule based on your time frame.

Feminist Analysis Circle and French Doors

The reading schedule in figure 2.4 indicates the breakdown of the text's correlating chapters. While reading independently according to the schedule, students could use the Feminist Analysis Circle (see figure 2.5) and Thematic Topics of Feminist Criticism (see figure 2.3) to prompt their thinking and

Week	*Jane Eyre* (with important event)	*Dark Companion*
1	Chapter 2: Red Room	Prologue & Chapter 1
2	Chapter 4: Defying Mrs. Reed	Chapters 2, 3, and 4
3	Chapter 7: Lowood Punishment	Chapters 5, 6, and 7
4	Chapter 9: Helen Dies	Chapters 8, 9, and 10
5	Chapter 12: Rochester's First Appearance	Chapters 11, 12, and 13
6	Chapters 13–14: Jane & Mr. Rochester's Conversations	Chapters 14 and 15
7	Chapter 15: Jane Saves Rochester From a Fire	Chapters 16 and 17
8	Chapter 20: Mr. Mason Gets Attacked	Chapters 18 and 19
9	Chapter 23: Mr. Rochester's Proposal	Chapters 20 and 21
10	Chapter 25: Dreaming of Babies	Chapters 22, 23, 24
11	Chapter 26: The Wedding	Chapters 25, 26, 27
12	Chapter 27: Jane Flees Thornfield	Chapters 28, 29, 30
13	Chapter 28: Jane Gets Taken in by the Rivers	Chapters 31, 32, 33
14	Chapter 34–35: St. John's Proposal	Chapters 34, 35, 36
15	Chapter 36–38: Jane's Return to Thornfield, End	Chapter 37 & Epilogue

Figure 2.4 Recommended Reading Guide. Created by authors.

annotate the text. Akin to the color-coding scheme used in the "Paper Matches" activity in the before reading section of this chapter, students should track recognized themes as they read, documenting them for future discussion.

Next, provide each student with a sheet of white computer paper. Create a French door four-flap foldable. There will be four flaps, one for each thematic topic. Students can use color-coded markers to label each flap accordingly. As they read, they can document textual evidence (sentences, words, phrases) that are particularly relevant to feminist topics and make notes about them inside each flap. These foldables, maintained throughout the readings of both texts, will be particularly useful during the after-reading debate activity.

Exploring Feminist Thematic Topics

After each section of reading, students could participate in small-group discussions drawing on textual evidence reflective of the feminist thematic topics. This activity will help students who have read a substantial amount of text

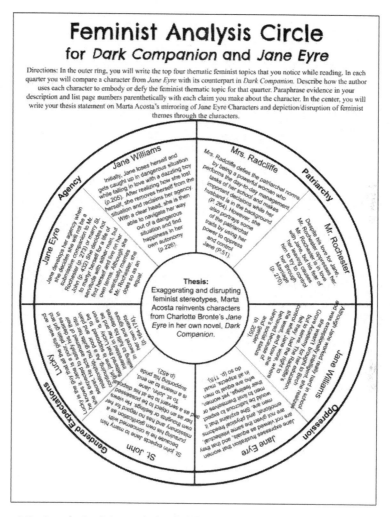

Feminist Analysis Circle
for *Dark Companion* and *Jane Eyre*

Directions: In the outer ring, you will write the top four thematic feminist topics that you notice while reading. In each quarter you will compare a character from *Jane Eyre* with its counterpart in *Dark Companion*. Describe how the author uses each character to embody or defy the feminist thematic topic for that quarter. Paraphrase evidence in your description and list page numbers parenthetically with each claim you make about the character. In the center, you will write your thesis statement on Marta Acosta's mirroring of Jane Eyre Characters and depiction/disruption of feminist themes through the characters.

Agency

Jane Williams
Initially, Jane loses herself and gets caught up in dangerous situation while falling in love with a dazzling boy (p.205). After realizing how she lost herself, she removes herself from the situation and reclaims her agency. With a clear head, she is then able to navigate her way out of a dangerous situation and find happiness in her own autonomy (p.226).

Jane Eyre
Jane develops her agency when she decides she will not be a submissive companion to Mr. Rochester (p. 273) or marry St. John (p. 452) She decides not to marry herself for a life of servitude with either man, but find herself and live on her own terms. Although she eventually marries Mr. Rochester, she does so as an equal.

Mrs. Radcliffe
Mrs. Radcliffe defies the patriarchal norms by being a powerful woman who perform the day-to-day management tasks of her school and makes important decisions while her husband is in the background (P. 264). However, she also portrays some traits of the patriarchal power to oppress and control Jane (P.51).

Patriarchy

Mr. Rochester
Despite his love for Jane, Mr. Rochester oppresses her with Jane, both his desire to control him to through Marriage. (p. 270).

Thesis:
Exaggerating and disrupting feminist stereotypes, Marta Acosta reinvents characters from Charlotte Bronte's *Jane Eyre* in her own novel, *Dark Companion*.

Jane Williams

Oppression

Jane Eyre

St. John
St. John expects Jane to marry him because he is seeking glorification with his missionary and has no regard for her thoughts or feelings. He views her as an object to be possessed. "To St. John, Jane is a servant to all his disposal, Burning his own glorification as a means to an end, It is a reflection of his pride (p. 452).

Lucky

Gendered Expectations

Figure 2.5   Sample Feminist Analysis Circle. Created by authors.

be able to talk about, discuss, and describe key themes by reducing down the text little by little until they can describe the selection (assigned chapters) in a single word. To begin, put students in teams of four and each will be assigned a theme to track individually: oppression, agency, gendered expectations, or patriarchy. Teams will be given a piece of chart paper that has been divided into four sections and color-coded for each theme. In the appropriate section, students will be responsible for recording textual evidence from the section to support one of the four studied feminist themes, tracking page numbers with powerful information in their assigned quadrants. To do this, students read the passage independently looking for a sentence they feel is particularly significant to a feminist theme. Next, students share their notes with the team and work collaboratively to extract a sentence or single phrase from their notes that aligned with their assigned theme. Finally, teams distill the sentence or phrase from each quadrant to single word from the readings that is significant to the feminist themes being discussed. This strategy, and text rendering, gives students opportunities to identify key details in the chapters, determine text importance, and collaboratively shape their understanding of the selections they read through a feminist lens. Advise students to take notes during the discussion for future reference.

After teams have completed the text rendering activity, they should be given one color-coded sticky note for each quadrant in order for team members to transfer each of their words to the appropriate color of the sticky note. Ask students to put all of their single rendered words (which are on sticky notes) onto the blank wall space or board in the classroom under the labeled theme. Once all words have been placed on these spaces, students should examine the words in each category and discuss what the author is implying about the theme based on the significant words they have pulled from the text. For example, when examining the category "oppression" the students might discuss the words and ask themselves, *What message is the author implying about the oppression of women? How do these words imply that theme?* Students should work together to create an evolving theme statement for the category. Students should continue discussion until they have addressed each category and started a theme statement for each.

Examining Character Counterparts

While reading and color-coding the text, students may be asked to connect the thematic topics in both texts by looking specifically at the characters. Using the Feminist Analysis Circle (figure 2.3), ask students to determine which characters in the novels are counterparts, or mirrors, of each other such as Mr. Rochester and Mrs. Radcliffe. In the outer ring of the circle, students will write the four thematic feminist topics they have been tracking throughout reading and discussion. In each quarter of the circle, students could compare a character from *Jane Eyre* with its counterpart in *Dark Companion*. Next, ask students to describe how the author uses each character to embody or defy the feminist thematic topic for that quarter. Students should be expected to paraphrase evidence in the description and list page numbers parenthetically with each claim about how the author uses each character to disrupt or depict the feminist topic in that quarter. In the center, students may write a thesis statement on Marta Acosta's mirroring of *Jane Eyre* characters and depiction and/or disruption of feminist themes through the characters.

AFTER READING

Before completing the after-reading activities, students should synthesize their understanding of the novels' feminist themes by completing a quick-write on the following question: *Which Jane better represents female agency and why?* This prewriting activity allows students to reflect upon connections between the protagonists and identified feminist themes before completing the class discussion and philosophical chairs debate.

Philosophical Chairs Debate

Students should be given another opportunity to talk about the two texts they have read. For this activity, you may pose a question in which listeners express two differing points of view. For example, you may say, "Which protagonist, Jane Eyre or Jane Williams, best exemplifies a strong female character who defies societal and/or gender expectations for her time period?" Students should then be given three to five minutes to independently write an opinion about the topic making sure to include supporting reasons and connections to themes.

Once students complete their quick-write, position them in two parallel lines facing each other—one on each side of the room, with one side supporting Jane Eyre and the other in favor of Jane Williams. Each side should discuss their reasoning and choose a spokesperson. During the philosophical chairs debate, the spokesperson from each team will face each other with their supporting members spread out behind them. Each spokesperson will have the opportunity to share the team's opening stance. Then, they should have about five minutes to reconvene to create a rebuttal for the opposite team's counterclaim. Each student will share a piece of evidence or reasoning with the spokesperson for this portion of the debate. Students may share the evidence in advance or pass notes to the spokesperson as needed during the debate. The spokesperson for each team will take turns sharing their evidence until all evidence has been shared. If class members are persuaded by one side's argument, they may switch sides at any time, but must contribute to that side's argument with new evidence. When the evidence has all been presented, the teacher calls a final vote and students will anonymously cast votes for the victor of their choice, Jane Eyre or Jane Williams. After the vote, students could write a paragraph reflecting how each Jane's character exemplifies each of the four feminist themes as a class exit ticket.

Found Poetry

Have students revisit their definitions of feminism from the pre-reading activities to recap what feminism is and how it shapes our understanding of the texts we read. Review the categories and evolving theme statements from the text rendering activity. Engage students in discussion by asking questions such as *How is the theme of oppression represented in Jane Eyre and Dark Companion? What scenes represent male dominant societies from each text? In both texts, women are only given power when they are responsible for caring for and educating children; how does this further contribute to your understanding of patriarchy and second-wave feminism? How do the*

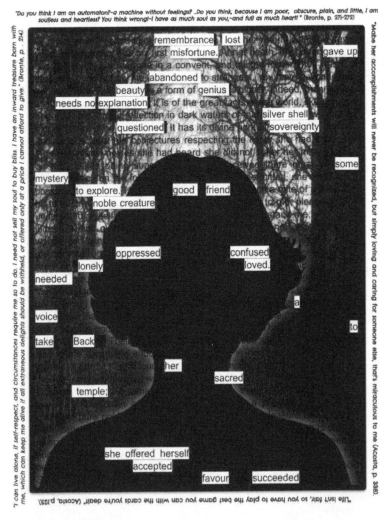

Figure 2.6 Digital Blackout Poem: Lost Autonomy, Power Reclaimed. Created by authors.

authors convince readers that Jane Eyre and Jane Williams *conform to or defy expectations for women in their time? How do the protagonists develop agency throughout the texts? How do these ideas modify or reinforce your understanding of feminism?*

To show their understanding of feminist themes, students can choose to create a form of found poetry known as the blackout poem. In this case, students could be given excerpts from the texts quoted at the beginning of each chapter in *Dark Companion*. The teacher can provide pages from these texts and allow students to choose a text sample from which to work. Students may also choose to start with a collage of quotes from *Jane Eyre* and *Dark Companion* instead. Ask students to think about a particular abstract noun or feminist thematic topic from the list in table 2.2. Then, ask them to write a thematic statement for this topic and use it to title their poem. From there, students may choose words in the original text to create a found poem that illustrates the particular feminist theme they chose from the novels. In essence, students will use a pencil to box in a selection of words on the page until they are satisfied with the resulting poem, which accurately represents their chosen theme. Next, students can pencil in artwork that symbolizes the feminist theme they have represented in words. Finally, students could use markers or paint—traditionally this is done with black, but any color is acceptable—to "blackout" or strategically cover the areas of the text where they do not want the words to be visible. The teacher could also ask students to provide textual evidence for their selected theme by "framing" their poem with three or four of the most compelling quotes from the text. Blackout poetry allows students to creatively show their understanding of a texts' feminist themes. Furthermore, this activity cultivates students' critical thinking and evaluation skills as they must find the words in a specific piece of text and order them so that they accurately represent the feminist theme they have chosen and support their assumptions with the strongest textual evidence. Another option is to complete the entire activity digitally using Google slides or Photoshop as in the example we have provided in figure 2.6.

EXTENSION ACTIVITES

As an opportunity for students to continue learning about the studied themes of gender, power, and class, we share sample extension activities that provide students with additional practice applying what they learned during the study of *Jane Eyre* and *Dark Companion*. In the following section, we outline how to extend and deepen student understanding of the primary characters in the studied texts including Mr. Rochester, Jane Eyre, Mrs. Reed, Mr. Brocklehurst, Mrs. Fairfax, and Saint John (*Jane Eyre* characters) and those main characters from *Dark Companion*: Jane Williams, Mrs. Radcliffe, Hattie, Jack, Lucky, and Mr. Mason.

Trading Cards

To begin, teachers could assign four or five students in the class to one of the aforementioned novel characters until each person in the class has been assigned a character to study. These small groups will then become experts of their assigned characters. During small group discussions, students will identify key characteristics of their assigned character, determine how their character contributed to feminist theories/frameworks previously studied, and use Read Write Think's interactive program, Trading Card Creator, to create a detailed character trading card. Students will be prompted to answer questions about their assigned characters' traits and upload images representing their characters. After answering all prompts and uploading images, downloadable trading cards will be generated (see figure 2.7).

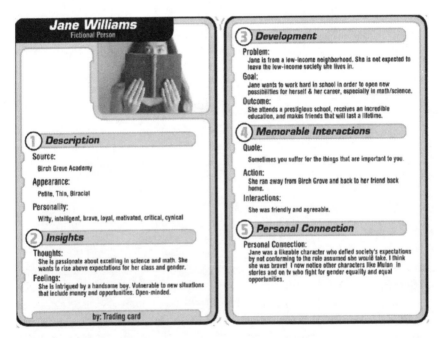

Figure 2.7 Sample Character Trading Card. Created by authors.

Looking to Hire

After character trading cards have been completed, students can work with their character teams to create a job advertisement for one of the following positions: headmistress at Birch Grove Academy (*Dark Companion*), tutor at Birch Grove Academy (*Dark Companion*), or governess at Thornton (*Jane Eyre*). Ask students to consider what they learned about marginalized voices, gendered stereotypes, norms, choice, and empowerment as they design the advertisement. Consider using an online tool for graphic design, such as Google Docs, to design the application collaboratively.

To extend this, students can participate in a role-play activity where they interview for one of the advertised jobs. Before beginning the activity, teachers should provide students with a list of sample interview questions: *Why are you interested in this position? What makes you a good candidate for this position? What personality trait makes you most valuable? What are three positive things others might say about you? How do you resolve conflict? How would you describe your work history?* One at a time, student representatives for each character team will be asked to sit in the front of the classroom for a hot seat interview. Simulating a mock interview for one of the job openings, audience members can ask the interviewee questions about why their character would be the best candidate for the job. The audience can take turns asking each character five questions until all characters have had a chance to be in the hot seat and they have asked all the interview questions they created. Students in the hot seat may use their character trading cards for reference while answering the interview questions. Critically thinking through the design of the job announcement and the process of being interviewed allows students opportunities to think through the critical feminist lens and apply that criticism to an authentic experience.

Spoken Word Poetry

Feminist pedagogy is not just learning what feminism is. Rather, it is about moving from knowing to doing, from listening to speaking, and from conforming to resisting. To truly deepen learning, students must take what they learned about feminism beyond the pages of the books. More than lessons in a classroom, their knowledge must impact the media they consume, the conversations they have, and the decisions they make.

Being able to confidently speak about social justice topics enables students to extend feminist discourse from a classroom to a space where authentic conversations with family and friends can take place, giving students an opportunity to advocate for change. To give students the chance to speak out on behalf of social justice issues that are important to them, students can research a feminist social justice issue and craft a reflection and commentary poem in the form of spoken word poetry. Based on their interests, students can choose a feminist social justice issue such as suffrage, education, representation, sexism, domestic assault, #metoo, workplace equality, or another approved feminist topic. Students should locate and read a minimum of two reliable and valid sources. Next, ask students to combine words from their sources with their own words to craft a spoken word poem that gives voice to the issue. Students should view feminist spoken word poetry exemplars and work with the teacher to craft a poem following these steps:

- Choose a subject you care about.
- Tell a story that shares your message.
- Use sensory language and literary devices to grab your reader.
- Read your poem aloud and edit it.
- Memorize your poem.
- Perform it.

Students should perform their project for the class, the school, and/or the community if possible. Or, students can record their performances and the teacher can compile all digital files into one presentation to share with the class or school community.

CONCLUSION

The strong female characters in *Dark Companion* and *Jane Eyre* rebel against gender norms and societal expectations in two vastly different time periods. In 19th-century England, Jane Eyre is expected to occupy a subservient role as an impoverished governess and caretaker for a wealthy proprietor, yet she defies the gender expectations of her time period to assert her independence and find her own version of happiness. Two hundred years later in the United States, Jane Williams, a poor orphan in a violent neighborhood, is expected to live on the streets and conform to the various illicit lifestyles of her peers; yet she leaves town and finds new opportunities for herself. Through this pairing, the ways in which women navigate oppression, agency, gendered expectations, and patriarchy in an ever-evolving society can be explored.

As students navigate sociopolitical and gender-charged information, providing complex, accessible, and relatable literature is important. Pairing texts such as *Jane Eyre* and *Dark Companion* provides opportunities for students to critically think about how women are depicted in texts, how women occupy particular gendered roles, and how women navigate a male-dominated society and begin asking questions about who holds the power and what they can do to disrupt these gendered norms.

REFERENCES

Bruce, H., Brown, S., McCracken, N. M., & Bell-Nolan, M. (2008). Feminist pedagogy is for everybody: Troubling gender in reading and writing. *English Journal, 97*(3), 82–89.

Crabtree, R. D., & Sapp, D. A. (2003). Theoretical, political, and pedagogical challenges in the feminist classroom. *College Teaching, 51*(4), 131–40.

DigitalGuru101. (2020a, June 23). *Vampires in film/TV* [Video]. YouTube. https://youtu.be/h4S9VI2guZk.

DigitalGuru101. (2020b, June 23). *Women in film* [Video]. YouTube. https://youtu.be/a5ftNIh4KA4.

Hesse-Biber, S. N. (2012). *Handbook of feminist research: Theory and praxis.* Thousand Oaks, CA: SAGE.

hooks, b. (2014). *Talking back: Thinking feminist, thinking black.* New York, NY: Routledge.

Kaufman, D. R., & Lewis, R. (2012). From course to dis-course: Mainstreaming feminist, pedagogical, methodological, and theoretical perspectives. In S. Nagy Hesse-Biber (Eds.), *Handbook of feminist research: Theory and praxis* (pp. 659–674). Thousand Oaks, CA: SAGE.

Kelly, C. J. (2017). *The personal is political.* Encyclopedia Britannica. https://www.britannica.com/topic/the-personal-is-political.

Chapter 3

Governed by Rules

Possibilities and Consequences in Wuthering Heights *and* The Hate U Give

Michael Macaluso and Kati Macaluso

It might seem as if setting is a kind of straightjacket and, in fact, it is. But you might also see it as a kind of river channel in a canyon. There are only certain directions things can go, but slightly different routes can be taken and different events can happen. Trying to navigate a new channel is possible and can bring conflict and problems. Going outside the river is not possible.

—Smith & Wilhelm, 2010, p. 71.

Pairing *Wuthering Heights* with *The Hate U Give* seems like a stretch. Upon first glance, these texts have little, if anything, in common. One was written in the 19th century and takes place in a secluded English countryside. The other takes place in the present time in an unnamed American city. One centers on an adolescent, African American girl and the racism her community endures while the other focuses on two white families of different social standing. Despite these stark differences, we see a great deal of promise in using these novels to explore the influence, possibilities, and determinants of *setting* as a dynamic literary device, one that drives conflict, action, and consequences.

Considering setting in this way may be different than the way in which it is typically taken up in classrooms. Traditionally, we tend to think about setting as a physical location, or the time, place, and milieu in which a story occurs—the Jazz Age of *The Great Gatsby*, the Mississippi River in *The Adventures of Huckleberry Finn*, the Puritan culture of *The Crucible*, or Thornfield Hall in *Jane Eyre*. When setting is utilized and understood in this way, it serves at the very least as an expositional role for the narrative, helping, at most, to set context for the reader. It provides the backdrop against which the text unfolds and from which students are able to draw conclusions about the excess of the 1920s, about an antebellum slave economy, America's Puritan past, and Victorian England. Although the "time and place" of a story are important to texts, there is a risk in limiting setting to these somewhat static domains. In particular, it can overlook what Smith and Wilhelm (2010) call the important psychological, human, and social aspects of setting that animate and give shape to characters' values and conflicts and can cause characters to behave in certain ways.

From this more social perspective, some settings "set" or determine rules for characters as well as the "systems of relationships" by which they act and behave throughout their respective stories. Setting, in other words, constitutes the "interactive space" or the set of relationships that deeply influences what—rules, behaviors, and/or expectations—can happen in a story and how characters respond to those happenings as part of the plot development. For example, the social dimension of setting helps to explain why characters chosen as tributes in *The Hunger Games* abide by the simple rule that they must kill or be killed. But their situation is much more complex, as they navigate the game board, sponsors, other tributes, and even the parameters of their District that have set them up to thrive or falter within the game itself.

Smith and Wilhelm's definition of setting—along with the quotation that opens this chapter—might seem, on the surface, overly deterministic. In other words, it may seem as though a character's actions are a direct result of the setting out of which the character is derived. To a certain extent, setting *is* deterministic. Writers are bound by the rules of the textual world they have invented. For the sake of this chapter, it is that definition of setting—setting as "rule setting" (Smith & Wilhelm, 2010, p. 71)—that we wish to pursue. For every context comprised not only of physical and temporal location, but also of people, conventions, and beliefs, there are ways of behaving, interacting, valuing, thinking, and speaking that are accepted (or not) as representations of particular identities. Setting, therefore, affords teachers a rich platform by which to explore identity as a socially constructed phenomenon, but also to investigate the socially oriented roots of conflict. Because setting is really about "rule-setting," conflict can be understood as a function or consequence of setting; when characters try to resist or change themselves in relation to the social "rules" of their setting, the plot turns or the story ends.

This chapter, animated by a framework of the social dimension of setting, pairs the canonical *Wuthering Heights*, the second most frequently referenced text on the AP English literature exam free-response question (Albert.io, 2020), with the popular young adult novel *The Hate U Give*. This chapter will use the social dimension of setting to highlight the complex identities of Starr Carter, Catherine Earnshaw, and Catherine Linton and to show how they must navigate and reconcile the rules of their respective settings in order to accept their complex identities. This focus on setting makes the unlikely, though complimentary, pairing of *Wuthering Heights* and *The Hate U Give* more applicable to readers' worlds and lives as readers themselves are forever negotiating their own distinct "settings" and identities.

Wuthering Heights by Emily Bronte

First published in 1847 under a male pseudonym, *Wuthering Heights* has been long acknowledged for its complexity, artistry, style, and sophistication. Its endearing, albeit dramatic and often brutal characters have only cemented its place in the canon of classic literature. Being one of a handful of canonical British texts authored by a woman, it has emerged as a reputable alternative to the white male perspective and tends to find its place in secondary British literature classrooms, traversing both Gothic and Victorian traditions, as well as many an AP literature and composition syllabus.

Known for its shifting frame narrative, its detailed and deliberate prose, and its symbolic and significant use of settings, *Wuthering Heights* remains a complex commentary on human nature, love, obsession, revenge, as well as tragedy and redemption. The novel fixates, to a certain extent, on Heathcliff, the character that narrator Lockwood knows only as his dour landlord and resident of Wuthering Heights at the start of the novel. Through the narration of Nelly, the longtime housekeeper of Thrushcross Grange, readers come to know Heathcliff as the dark-skinned orphan boy adopted by the father of Catherine Earnshaw, a source of both love and rejection in Heathcliff's life. The novel chronicles the lives and intersections of two families, the Earnshaws of Wuthering Heights and the seemingly more refined Lintons of Thrushcross Grange, offering a commentary throughout on the complications that arise when love, the desire for social advancement, and the constraints of social rules and expectations come into conflict.

The Hate U Give by Angie Thomas

Written at the height of the #BlackLivesMatter movement, *The Hate U Give* was one of the first young adult novels to tackle the issue of police brutality against young African Americans. With the simple message of speaking up against injustice, the novel weaves issues of whiteness, racism, privilege, and systemic oppression into the story of a 16-year-old African American girl, Starr Carter, who witnesses the shooting of her good friend. Over the course of the novel, Starr must face the competing narratives and expectations of her poor, "ghetto" neighborhood Garden Heights and the "bougie" private school in the suburbs that her parents make her attend: Williamson Prep. Terrified of the two places ever colliding, Starr tries to maintain a distinct identity within each, but the shooting forces her to reevaluate that balance.

The range of complex characters, from Starr's reformed father to her white boyfriend, has made this novel a relatable text to readers of all races and ages and has slowly earned its way into secondary classrooms, if only as a summer reading assignment. Winner of number of awards, including the Coretta Scott King Award and inspired by the words of Tupac Shaker, *The Hate U Give* was recently named one of the most influential books of the decade by CNN.

BEFORE READING

Considering Social Settings

Given the importance of the social dimensions of setting to our reading of *Wuthering Heights* and *The Hate U Give*, students should be encouraged to delineate and describe their social environments and how their language, behavior, and expression may shift depending on the role they occupy or the people, expectations, and values that comprise a particular space. Some possible spaces to consider include home, school, church, a sporting event, dance practice, a friend's house on a Saturday night, workplace, and so on. Students should consider times when they have acted in accordance with the accepted values and expectations (i.e., "rules") of a particular group of people or space, as well as times they have felt themselves come into conflict with—or acted in opposition to—those values and expectations. A simple anticipatory set of questions should suffice to get them thinking about their social environments and the ways that certain groups, roles, and conventions might serve to limit or encourage types of behaviors and expectations. We imagine students answering these questions for homework, sharing in small groups in class the next day, and then debriefing as a large group. The large group discussion should converge around the ideas that students frequently change their behaviors and actions (their identities) depending on what they are doing (roles), where they are (space), why they act a certain way (expectations), and how they are expected to act (norms). Questions may include the following:

- **Thinking about Roles:** What is expected of you when you attend a sporting event as a spectator versus as a player? How might your behaviors, actions, and mindset be different despite being in the same physical place?
- **Thinking about Spaces:** How does your parent, guardian, sibling, or friend act with you while at home? What are some things they may expect of and allow for while in the comfort of your homes? How might these same people act differently or expect differently of you if you were to visit

them at their place of work or at school? What accounts for this change between the two scenarios?

- **Thinking about Expectations:** Though they are both formal events, how might you act differently at your school's graduation ceremony compared to a funeral? Why is this the case? Do you bring these certain expectations to those places/events or do those places/events expect certain behaviors of you?
- **Thinking about Cultural Norms:** How might a male client be received at a nail salon in a small town in the Southern United States versus a nail salon in Manhattan? What cultural expectations of maleness are accounted for (and why?) as we shift from one imagined scenario to the next?

These questions will prime students to think about the ways people act differently depending on roles, spaces, expectations, and norms.

For example, in response to these questions, students will realize that being a fan at a sporting event holds them accountable to fewer behavioral standards than the players on the field. When the umpire calls a strike for a pitch that was clearly outside the boundaries of Homeplate, a fan might break out in a fit of rage and still remain in her seat. Meanwhile, if the batter were to have the same reaction, he might find himself in the dugout for the rest of the game. In other words, same ballpark, same game, but different roles, so different rules. Likewise, students might acknowledge that an encounter with a close friend or parent at their place of work, as opposed to their home, may have felt odd because their parent or friend had to act more reserved than usual. They could not be as affectionate or as jocular, for example, because they were expected to behave more professionally in their place of work. Students will likely be able to recall instances in which they may have called a parent/ guardian at work, finding that their mother's typically more-than-audible "I love you" sounds a bit more muted from the confines of her office.

While it seems obvious, students can articulate that certain events—like a funeral or graduation ceremony—carry different expectations for behavior. Astute students may recognize that these very different events may call for similar attire and/or group of relatives or friends even though they stem from entirely different reasons or motivations for convening. Another example that might help to elaborate the point at the core of this third question about expectations is that of professional golf versus professional football. Though both fall within the realm of professional sports, and both are typically played outdoors, the expectations of fans attending a professional golf tournament include relatively formal attire and silence from the gallery. Meanwhile, a t-shirt and sweatpants will get a fan into a professional football game without a second thought, and signs demanding, "Make some noise!" flash across the jumbotron throughout the game.

Lastly, the final example should be handled delicately, so as not to inadvertently reinforce stereotypes, but the point here is that norms for behavior can also serve as rules by which we behave and are judged by others. The goal with this nail salon example is to encourage students to think through broad societal norms associated with an identity category like gender and the contexts that may bend those norms. In this case, while nail salons may be femininely gendered, it might be perfectly common to see high-profile men of New York City attentive to their appearance patron a salon for a manicure. At the same time, it might be just as common to be surprised at the sight of a man in a nail salon in a small Southern town of United States, where traditional values and behaviors may be expected and encouraged. With these scenarios, students will have to grapple with gender norms as rules that fluctuate from one context to another.

Through these examples, students should begin to think critically about the role(s) they have been cast into by the social circumstances and norms, and they will begin to unpack the typically assumed and often invisible theories about what counts as the "normal" or "accepted" ways of thought, expression, and behavior in and across varying social contexts. Teachers, then, can use these examples to directly introduce the concept of implicit or explicit "rule-setting" that occurs across roles, spaces, expectations, and norms. This will be immediately followed with the next activity, where the social dimension of setting is formally introduced as one of three elements or aspects of setting. Though the primary objective of this pre-reading exercise is to make students aware that a key dimension of setting is the rules that govern viable social participation, these anticipatory questions may also tee up a focal thought exercise after teaching the novels: students might begin to think about the ways they themselves juggle hybrid and possibly even conflicting identities depending upon where and with whom they are interacting.

Nuancing Setting

Having primed students to think about social rules as an essential dimension of setting, teachers may begin to break apart setting beyond its strictly physical or temporal (time-related, for example, time era or time duration) construct. We have modeled this effectively with students and teachers using a simple organizer and some accessible texts, as illustrated in figure 3.1.

Since students will likely be familiar with the typical physical and temporal dimensions of setting, we start with a simple image of a haunted house and invite students to identify the physical characteristics of the house and its surroundings. Some of them may even begin to note the mood or tone of the picture as a result of their insight into the physical condition of the setting.

Dimensions of Setting	Text	Definition and Examples
Physical	a haunted house	<u>Definition</u>: Physical location, attributes, or geography <u>Examples</u>: isolated on a hill, dilapidated porch, cobwebs
Temporal	"Story of an Hour" *The Tale of the Three Brothers* *The Great Gatsby* *The Crucible*	<u>Definition</u>: The duration of time in which the narrative unfolds; the time period in which the narrative is set. <u>Examples</u>: Chopin's "Story of an Hour" takes place in a single hour. *The Tale of the Three Brothers* speaks to the influence of the past on the present. *The Great Gatsby* takes place in the Jazz Age, and *The Crucible* takes place in the Puritan witch-hunt era.
Social	Super Smash Brothers *The Lego Movie* intro	<u>Definition</u>: The "interactive space" (Wilhelm and Smith, 2010) of setting. <u>Examples</u>: To successfully navigate the Super Smash brothers game board, a player has to know how the characters interact with the space and objects that comprise the board. To thrive in the Lego world, individuals must abide by a range of rules and expectations.

Figure 3.1   Different Dimensions of Setting. Created by authors.

Likewise, to discuss the importance that time can play in a text, we have reviewed familiar texts that center around the passage of time (like *The Story of an Hour* or *The Tale of the Three Brothers* from *Harry Potter*) or that take place during a specific era. In both cases, time lends insight into characters' conflicts and their ultimate evolution.

There are a variety of examples teachers can utilize to delve into the social aspects of setting. Most dystopian texts display a rich social dimension of setting, where a character will resist the rules of the dystopian society to bring about change. With most students proving familiar with at least some dystopian settings (like *The Hunger Games*), teachers can discuss specific examples of characters testing, questioning and even violating the rules of the social worlds they inhabit. For the sake of time and simplicity, one suggestion is to use the introduction from *The Lego Movie* (on YouTube) to offer clear and practical insight into the rules of the Lego world and how those rules clearly set up a future conflict for the main character within the first minutes of the film, reinforcing the idea that conflict is a function of setting.

In this short introduction, we learn through the main character, Emmett, that citizens of the Lego world have a series of instructions for "fitting in" to society, like greeting their neighbors, rooting for the local sports team, participating in Taco Tuesday, and drinking overpriced coffee. These rules do more than just reinforce the community building; they actually determine or control how characters behave, with clear consequences for those who don't. These rules foreshadow the impending conflict of Emmett "breaking the rules" of conformity and challenging the interactive space of the Lego world. Having students identify these rules and consider Emmett's relationship to these rules and his Lego world sets the stage for students to understand setting beyond time and place.

Once the social aspect of setting is introduced to students, they should immediately begin to see how this concept resonates with other texts and even their own lives. By posing the simple questions *What other texts can you think of where characters act according to certain rules? and Are there examples from your own life?* students can brainstorm examples worthy of consideration for class discussion. For example, one of our students noted how the rules of the Lego world in *The Lego Movie* resemble some of the things they do in order to "fit in" with peers. Another referenced *Super Smash Brothers*, a video game where characters must battle each other while navigating the ever-changing stage or board. Characters can just as easily be defeated by the disastrous elements of the board ("the setting") as they can by other characters. Other students have mentioned popular media like *Stranger Things* or *Jumanji*, both cases where characters must be mindful of abiding by the "rules" of certain "interactive spaces" (e.g., the Upside Down of *Stranger Things*, the game world of *Jumanji*) in order to survive and/or overcome challenges. A discussion of pop culture texts like these will surface the important and dynamic aspects of the social dimension of setting as they begin their closer readings of *Wuthering Heights* and *The Hate U Give*.

DURING READING

Given the investment in the social dimension of setting because of what it affords in terms of illuminating characters' complexities and conflict, we recommend an almost ethnographic reading of *Wuthering Heights* and *The Hate U Give*—giving as much attention to the setting as one gives the characters. We recommend some close-reading activities to support students' analysis of the role the various settings play with the female protagonists of each text. In both novels, these characters feel torn between multiple worlds and the person(s) or identity(ies) that both worlds require of them, essentially creating double identities for each of the novels' female protagonists. One key difference is that, by the end of the novels, Starr and Catherine Linton are able to reconcile their multiple worlds within a single identity. Catherine Earnshaw, on the other hand, is unable to do so and, in choosing a setting that defies an essential part of her nature, she dies an untimely death.

Setting's Effect on Character

This during-reading activity focuses on an in-depth comparative analysis of the main female characters in their respective settings that persists over the entirety of both texts. To track the characters' shifting thoughts and actions as they negotiate these settings, we suggest using a table like the one below, allowing students to keep a running record as they read. figure 3.2 offers an in-depth look at Starr in the first couple of chapters of the book, highlighting her interactions with the rules of her settings. Importantly, after a failed sleepover with friends who didn't want to spend the night in "the ghetto," Starr realizes her distinct settings from a young age. She reflects, "That's when I realized Williamson is one world and Garden Heights is another, and I have to keep them separate" (p. 36). Figure 3.2 can help students see the characteristics of these distinct settings and how Starr deals with them.

Dueling Houses

In using a similar setup with *Wuthering Heights*, students can see how Starr's story parallels that of Catherine Earnshaw (Cathy I) and Catherine Linton (Cathy II). We suggest using either the same table format for Cathy I and Cathy II or one like figure 3.3 to more robustly capture how the competing houses call for and mirror a personality or identity that befits the house, an intentional feature of the first half of the book. This way, students can see the social dimensions of setting at play. The inhabitants of the stormy Wuthering Heights house tend to be spirited, wild, passionate, and emotional, and freely given to "violent dispositions" reminiscent of Gothic/ Romantic qualities (p. 119), while those of the stately Thrushcross Grange manor tend to be more refined, reserved, domestic, and sophisticated and,

Starr	
THUG begins with Starr's comment: "There are just some places where it's not enough to be me. Either version of me" (p. 3). What do these different versions of Starr look like? How does she feel the need to act or behave as these versions at each of the places below? Cite page numbers as you take notes.	
at Garden Heights	At Williamson Prep
• Feels an allegiance the Garden • Can be confrontational (p. 71) • Has to earn "coolness" (p. 11) • Has some street credibility because of her father (p. 17) • Has to act a certain way around cops (p. 20) • Can freely speak slang and rap (p. 71)	• "I just wish I could be myself at Williamson…" (p. 35). • Needs to be approachable, reserved, nonconfrontational (p. 71) • "cool black kid" (p. 11); "representative" (p.186) • Avoid being the "Angry Black Girl" or "Weak Black Girl" (p. 115) • Aware of language and speech so as not to sound "ghetto" or "hood" (pp. 71, 95).

Figure 3.2 Starr's Social Worlds. Created by authors.

Wuthering Heights	Thrushcross Grange
Describe the physical features of the house (location, appearance, etc.) from Chapters 1-2: • Isolated, removed (p. 1) • Surrounded by thorns and "straggling" weeds/bushes (p. 6) • Hard earth; black frost • Large, jutting stones • Narrow windows • Hilltop, exposed to and impacted by "tumultuous" weather (p. 2) • Ornate carvings and statues; dark, dismal (p. 11)	**Describe the physical features of the house (location, appearance, etc.) from Chapter 6:** • Bright, full of lights – like "heaven" (p. 42) • In the middle of lush park in a valley (p. 42), surrounded by manicured hedges, flower pots, and a stone wall • Beautiful, splendid, shimmering, soft • Crimson, gold, white interior (p. 42)
Describe the people of the house (Heathcliff, Hareton, Hindley, Joseph): • Wild, passionate, emotional, spirited, rough, savage, icy, heartless (p. 4)	**Describe the people of the house (Nelly, Isabella, Edgar, Mrs. Linton):** • Refined, sophisticated, domestic, reserved, spoiled (p.43)
What is Cathy I like while she's at this house over the next several chapters? • Selfish, elitist, harsh • "She never had the power to conceal her passion." (p. 64)	What is Cathy I like while she's at this house over the next several chapters? • Behaved, affectionate but still emotional, passionate, and elitist • "It was not the thorn bending to the honeysuckles, but the honeysuckles embracing the thorn." (p. 83)
Inference questions: • Which house does Cathy I prefer? Explain. • Which "lifestyle" or personality seems more reflective of Cathy I's identity? Explain. • Which house and lifestyle seem to be more dominant than the other?	

Figure 3.3. The Social Dimension of Setting in *Wuthering Heights*. Created by authors.

thus, more Victorian in nature. Importantly, though, the last section of this organizer asks students to reflect, much like we suggest they do with Starr's character in *The Hate U Give*, on Cathy I and the way she changes across these two worlds.

Using this table format and prompts, students should be able to recognize a key difference between Starr and Cathy: Cathy I is unable to reconcile her competing social settings and personalities. She instead feels stifled by the life she has chosen—that of Thrushcross Grange, the Lintons, and Edgar—as evidenced by her behavior in Chapter 12. She tears open pillows, loosens her constraining clothes, lets down her hair, and calls out from an open window in the middle of winder, "Oh, I'm burning! . . . Why am I so changed? Why does my blood rush into a hell of tumult at a few words? I'm sure I should be myself were I once among the heather on those hills [at Wuthering Heights] . . . Heathcliff . . . I won't rest until you are with me . . ." (p. 115). Soon after, she dies.

Character Studies

Before or after important scenes in the novels, students can delve more deeply into the differing identities of the characters in a more meaningful way to predict what is to come next in the plot or to review these characters at key scenes. To help students visualize and keep track of characters' multiple, and sometimes conflicting, identities, we recommend providing them with a simple tracing of a human figure that they are able to fold lengthwise down the middle. Having students use the template to keep notes about the characters at key moments of conflict and character development will assist them in analyzing how these characters negotiate their identities and settings—what Starr refers to as "flipping the switch" (p. 71). More specifically, Catherine Linton (Cathy II) and Starr manage to embrace the best of both of their settings/identities, allowing them to reconcile the rules and to be at peace with their place and position.

For example, using this graphic organizer towards the end of *The Hate U Give*, immediately before the beginning of Part 5, students can log the dueling identities of Starr but then to see how her participation in the protest actually brings together these two sides for the first time. As a result of her participation, she realizes that "things will never be the way they used to be" (p. 433), that "we ain't gotta live [at Garden Heights] to change things . . . We just gotta give a damn" (p. 436), and that she is no longer ashamed of her attachment to Garden Heights (p. 441). These are key realizations. Teachers can also use this same figure to have students conduct analyses of the complex identities of several other characters, like Uncle Carlos, DeVante, Khalil, Seven, and Maverick, as they navigate and negotiate the rules of their different settings over the course of the novel as well. For example, students tend to be fascinated with Uncle Carlos, a black police officer who initially defends the police officer who shot Khalil. Rather than seeing him as a one-sided figure that's often depicted in news headlines, they see Uncle Carlos as someone with conflicting obligations to his police squad and family, neighborhood and duty, and race and occupation. The same can be said for Maverick, who is given a detailed backstory that showcases his gangster former life up against his reformed lifestyle.

Likewise, using this figure with the latter half of *Wuthering Heights* can leave students well-poised to see how Cathy II grows into a disposition that embraces the qualities of both settings. From Chapter 18, Nelly notes how Cathy II retains the best and worst qualities of her parents: high spirit, soft, mild, and gentle with a deep and tender affection but saucy and often cross and snotty. By the start of this section of the novel, she looks down upon her cousin Hareton as a brute servant, but by the end of this section, she comes around to him, sees how they complement each other, and even asks forgiveness of Hareton for the way she has treated him in the past. Nelly comments on this complementary nature when she says in Chapter 32, "The intimacy [between Cathy II and Hareton] thus commenced, grew rapidly . . . both their minds tending to the same point—one loving and desiring to esteem, and the other loving and desiring to be esteemed " (p. 289). In fact, they recognize that these qualities were always "in" them, but that the conditions of each place magnified, at times, the worst of those qualities. Thus, Cathy II and Hareton—through their union (something denied to Cathy I when she chose Edgar over Heathcliff)—are able to balance the rules called for from both houses.

Similarly, while Starr sees Williamson Prep as an escape from her Garden Heights background, the events of the novel illustrate how she cannot avoid her Garden Heights home. In addition to coming to terms with—and standing up against—the racial violence that has happened with her community, she realizes that her Williamson friends and boyfriend can never really know her unless they also know about her Garden Heights background and personality, something she has desperately tried to conceal while at school. Ultimately, her decision to stand up and protest allows her to embrace her Garden Heights personality—both at home and at Williamson. Thus, the novel is not just about Starr finally being able to participate in the Garden Heights protests, but also about coming to terms with multiple dimensions of her identity. By the end of the novel, her friends and family know Starr as someone who can traverse both settings and whose personality is informed by both communities, rather than one or the other.

AFTER READING

"Pulling It All Together" Questions

After reading both *Wuthering Heights* and *The Hate U Give*, students should be prepared to generate claims about the relationship between character and setting, in particular with respect to the ways that setting influences characters' actions and behaviors. Students should also, as anticipated by the pre-reading activities, be able to elaborate the ways that characters find themselves navigating multiple settings, negotiating identities across those settings. While these questions do not necessarily call for one correct answer, some suggested responses are included.

What is the relationship between character and setting?

Setting can greatly affect character motivation and development by establishing the rules by which a character will conflict or acquiesce. We see this in a text like *The Crucible*, where characters subscribe to certain ideologies and act in accordance with or against herd mentalities. Racism, as depicted in *The Hate U Give*, acts similarly, with some characters, like Hailey, dismissing racism and others, like Starr and even Chris, calling it out and working against it.

How does setting determine or influence
characters' actions and behaviors?

Setting can be deterministic in that the social rules, expectations, and/or norms of the setting setup probable decisions, actions, and/or behaviors for characters. For example, the house of Wuthering Heights seemed to bring out the worst in its inhabitants, reducing characters like Heathcliff and Hindley to violent brutes at times. Further, Cathy I's decision to marry Edgar was motivated in part by her allure for a grander lifestyle; she desired the loftier way of living at the Grange, and the benefits that came with it, than with her own position, which still boasted a comfortable lifestyle. Cathy II, on the other hand, learned to defy the snobbish expectations of her house with her love for Hareton.

How do characters navigate multiple settings? How do they (or
do they not) negotiate their identity(ies) across these settings?

Negotiating setting is about identity-building or identity-breaking. Acclimating to the rules of a certain setting shows membership and even assimilation. Both novels feature main characters who try to balance their setting-informed identities, and this is a common these in many texts. For example, in *The Absolutely True Diary of a Part-Time Indian*, Junior also tries to navigate the rules and expectations with his new, upper-class white school and his Reservation. The major plot of the novel shows him trying to negotiate these very different settings and identities.

What happens when characters try to resist the rules of a setting
or try to acclimate to the interactive space of a setting that does
not resonate with their values, interests, beliefs, or personality?

In these cases, conflict happens, and it can lead to disastrous results, like Cathy I, as its akin to denying your true self or identity. Conversely, it can lead to a reconciliation of sorts, like it did with Starr and Cathy II, where characters come to terms with their setting or construct a new identity that rectifies their competing identities.

Critical Lenses

In addition to a detailed look at setting and the main female characters of the novel, pairing *Wuthering Heights* with *The Hate U Give* also offers comparable readings through a number of other topics, themes, and lenses, including masculinity (Hindley, Edgar, Heathcliff, Linton, Hareton, DeVante, Chris, Carlos, Maverick), postcolonialism and race, class, family ties and values, and even love and loss. Students can reenter the text with one of these lenses to make a comparative analysis across the two texts and specific characters, noting how the rules of cultural norms and expectations play a role in how the characters act, in establishing conflict, and in influencing how, if at all, characters navigate conflict resolution. Classrooms particularly attuned to social justice issues may find these lenses welcome, as they encourage readers to draw connections between these larger themes and their newfound understanding of the social dimension of setting, noting that this dimension need not be exclusively role or place-based (like a parent, student, house, neighborhood, or school). Indeed, ideologies and cultural expectations also

Lens	Guiding Question
Gender/Masculinity	• What expectations of masculinity is expected of the men of the novels? • How do the various male characters act differently and what accounts for those differences? • Which male characters are the most similar and which are the most different across the two texts? • Are any male characters required to balance different social settings? If so, how do they rectify them?
Race/Postcolonialism	• In what ways does race also act as an "interactive space," accounting for the ways in which people are expected to act, behave, and respond to others? • Does it matter that Heathcliff could have been a different race than the Earnshaws and/or Lintons (theories have been speculated about his race, with reference to his darker appearance and gypsy origins)? How do Chris and Starr deal with misunderstandings about each other and even with others' perceptions of their mixed-race relationship?
Class	• How are varying elements of socioeconomic class depicted across the two texts? • What types of behaviors are associated with those of a higher socioeconomic class versus those of a lower class? • How do characters like Starr and Cathy I deal with or respond to the different socioeconomic classes they traverse?
Family Values	• How do family expectations across the two texts shape characters' actions and behaviors? • In what ways do the characters resist or fulfill family values?
Love and Loss	• How do characters across both text deal with the loss of loved ones? Does one text offer a more "acceptable" form of loss? • How do characters express or show their love, whether romantic or platonic? In what ways do these texts make a comment on appropriate forms of platonic and romantic love?

Figure 3.4.   Extension Lenses for Examining Ideology as Setting. Created by authors.

constitute an interactive space or system of rules grounded in ideologies, systemic oppression, and privilege and marginalization that can dictate the ways in which individuals act, behave, and believe. Some guiding questions from these perspectives may include those listed in the figure 3.4.

For example, class and classism play a major role in both texts. Starr, Cathy I, and Cathy II all act certain ways because of their social positions. Starr feels inadequate around her Williamson friends and boyfriend because they travel to exotic places and live in bigger, fancier houses (pp. 76, 81). This feeling of inadequacy affects the way she acts around them, but she ultimately comes to terms with this feeling and feels pride in her Garden Heights home. Cathy I, on the other hand, is completely motivated by class. In one of the most important scenes of the book, she reveals to her housekeeper that it "would degrade [her] to marry Heathcliff" (p. 73) despite her intense love for him. She chooses, instead, to marry Edgar because "he will be rich, and I shall like to be the greatest woman of the neighborhood" (p. 71). Cathy fails to foresee, however, that she will be unable to acclimate to Edgar's lifestyle and to completely deny her love of Heathcliff. Cathy II, born and bred in the upper-class lifestyle of Thrushcross Grange, eventually builds a new identity with lowly Hareton Earnshaw. Both of these characters previously despised each other for their behaviors associated with their social classes: Hareton found Cathy to be saucy, while Cathy thought Hareton uncultivated (p. 276). They eventually come around to each other, though, constructing a new identity together with "both their minds tending to the same point" (p 289). Starr and Cathy II prove that while class can be a determining factor of behavior, it need not be entirely determinate or deleterious.

EXTENSION ACTIVITIES

Analyzing Other Texts

Having analyzed the word through a close reading of *Wuthering Heights* and *The Hate U Give*, students will be well-poised to analyze their world through that same lens. Students should be able to take the tool of the social dimension of setting and analyze another text or set of texts for evidence of setting as a conglomeration of social rules and how those rules give shape to and arise from multiple identities. For example, they may consider analyzing popular movies or TV shows (e.g., *Spiderman: Into the Spiderverse*, *Stranger Things*, *The Crown*, or *The Marvelous Mrs. Maisel*), prominent celebrities or politicians (e.g., Meghan Markle or Selena Gomez), or even their own contexts or other family members (e.g., parents at home vs. parents at work) for the ways in which these individuals have to balance the different social settings of their lives. Students may learn that these individuals are actually strategic in how they live and act in these settings in order to balance them successfully.

To more thoroughly illustrate these social rules, teachers can use the inaugural episode of *The Crown* to capture one of Elizabeth's defining conflicts over the course of the series: the constraints placed on her family, her freedom, and her own passions by the rules of royalty. This illustration lends credence to regular headlines about the struggles of the royal family as they navigate these rules. Another text popular with students is the movie *The Greatest Showman*. The main idea of the entire movie can be explained through the social dimension of setting, seeing as P. T. Barnum recruits for his circus act people who do not follow, abide by, or conform to social norms, expectations, and roles. The "world" of his circus allows a space for these people-turned-performers to construct their own rules and norms. As one of the performers eventually sings in the movie's signature song, "This is Me," "I won't let them break me down to dust/I know that there's a place for us/ For we are glorious . . ." The circus is not just a "space" where they can be accepted but a place where—by revising the rules—they can act, behave, and live freely outside of society's rigid conventions.

While it might be obvious to see how the social dimension of setting works with a character like the bearded woman, teachers can share the song "The Other Side" from the movie musical to nuance the difficulties of breaking one's implied social rules. In this song, P. T. Barnum tries to convince social-ite Phillip Carlyle to fund and join his circus, telling him, "I can cut you free/ Out of the treachery and walls you keep in . . . come with me and take the ride . . . [or] Stay in the cage," noting the conventional and strict rules of high society that Phillip must follow. In initially rejecting Barnum's offer, Carlyle replies, "I quite enjoy the life you say I'm trapped in . . . I live among the swells . . . I'm okay with this uptown part I get to play." It's easy to pass off this conversation as classist—the elite Carlyle resisting involvement with the lower-class dealings of Barnum; however, implied in their sentiments is an acknowledgment of the *parts they play* because of their social class and soci-etal expectations. In this sense, their choices, actions, and behavior are some-what determined by their social situation. Carlyle also suggests that there are consequences for breaking these rules, when he sings, "If I were mixed up with you, I'd be the talk of the town/Disgraced and disowned, another one of the clowns. . ." This scene and the rest of the movie illustrate the very real influences and effects of the social dimension of setting on characters.

Analyzing Their Own Lives

In addition to having the opportunity to analyze texts other than *Wuthering Heights* and *The Hate U Give*, students should revisit the questions that began this unit as part of the pre-reading activities. These more general questions asked students about their lives and contexts, but now, with a more thorough understanding of the social dimension of setting, they can approach these questions—and their lives—with a more nuanced lens. In revisiting these questions, teachers should ask students how they now see the social aspect of setting embedded in these questions and, with this in mind, if they may think differently about their initial responses.

To dive even more concretely into their own lives, students—as a way of punctuating their analysis of setting across both *Wuthering Heights* and *The Hate U Give*—could now read the "text" of their lives at school for evidence of rule-setting. *How is school (like the settings of* Wuthering Heights *and* The Hate U Give*) comprised of multiple settings that, together, cast into view people's multiple identities, as well as the real-world possibilities and conflicts available to human beings?* Students may consider, for example, the distribution of demographics across multiple spaces in their high school. One of our students, for example, analyzed racial distribution across three spaces: the varsity basketball team's practice, the cafeteria at lunchtime, and the third period AP biology class. In each of these spaces, this student—himself an African American in a majority white school—noted a majority black presence on the Varsity team, a minority presence in the AP biology class, and an equal, but segregated, presence in the cafeteria, attributing these different distributions to the unspoken rules of the school. Likewise, students may recognize the unspoken rules of the cafeteria—not those about the efficiency and cleanliness of the lunchroom—but those that can determine who sits and eats where or how they are supposed to act around their peers versus in their classroom desks within the proximity of their teachers. One of our students noted the different, and again unspoken, behavioral expectations across some teachers' classrooms depending on the teachers' teaching and management styles. Students obviously behaved better for those teachers who had more rules or demanded higher expectations. These examples show how something as simple as one's school burdens students with multiple, and even differing, expectations.

CONCLUSION

This chapter offers quite a bit of analytic possibility in using the social aspect of setting to think through *Wuthering Heights* and *The Hate U Give*. Indeed, a deep analysis of this social dimension, as seen through actual locations like houses or through systems of beliefs like racist or classist ideologies, illuminates the possibilities and consequences available to characters (and, by extension, their authors) when they follow, break, manipulate, negotiate, and/or cross the distinct rules that govern them. As such, students can see the setting as something more than just expositional "time and place"—a literary device with practice and real-world implications.

On that note, we agree with Smith and Wilhelm when they say, "context is essential to an understanding of any human activity or achievement, both in reading and in our lives" (2010, p. 110). If the teaching of English is governed by the rule of world and word, then an understanding of setting is vital to any reader's real and literary lives. For understanding social settings allows them to see what's possible and to make sense of their own and other's actions and decisions, successes and failures, and manipulations and compliance as discreet or conspicuous acts of identity-making.

REFERENCES

Albert.io. (2020, April 21). The ultimate AP English literature reading list. Retrieved from https://www.albert.io/blog/ultimate-ap-english-literature-reading-list/.

Brontë, E. (1981/1870). *Wuthering heights*. New York, NY: Bantam Books.

Smith, M. W., & Wilhelm, J. D. (2010). *Fresh takes on teaching literary elements: How to teach what really matters about character, setting, point of view, and theme*. New York, NY: Scholastic.

Thomas, A. (2017). *The hate u give*. New York, NY: HarperCollins Publishers.

Chapter 4

"I Wish I Weren't so High"

Substance Abuse and Addiction in We Were Liars *and* The Great Gatsby

Janine Darragh

Though written nearly 90 years apart, F. Scott Fitzgerald's (1925) *The Great Gatsby* and E. Lockhart's (2014) *We Were Liars* have a multitude of similarities. From displays of opulent wealth and characters who arguably struggle with substance abuse, addiction, and emotional wellness, these two novels offer ample opportunities for students to explore the timelessness of various issues which always have been and continue to be complex parts of the human experience. This chapter will share opportunities for pairing *The Great Gatsby* with *We Were Liars*, specifically using *The Great Gatsby* as an introduction to Lockhart's text in order to examine substance abuse and its impacts on individuals, families, communities, and the arts.

The Great Gatsby by F. Scott Fitzgerald

Against a 1920s' New York backdrop, F. Scott Fitzgerald's (1925) classic, *The Great Gatsby*, explores themes of wealth, opulence, and the pursuit of the American Dream. Narrator Nick Carraway moves to New York in 1922 to seek employment selling bonds. Reconnecting with his cousin, Daisy Buchanan, he finds himself drawn into the life and drama of the elite, "old money" dwellers of the East Egg. As the novel progresses, Nick tracks his summer in the city, specifically focusing on his neighbor, Jay Gatsby, who lives in an extravagant mansion and throws grand, excessive parties. Nick later learns that Gatsby is not who he says he is. Shrouded in mystery and connected to a variety of unsavory businesspeople, it becomes apparent that Gatsby is a self-made man, whose pursuit of one Daisy Buchanan has inspired his quest for wealth and beautiful things.

Throughout the course of this drama-filled novel, readers witness all the corruption surrounding the characters in the book. Tom Buchanan, a white supremacist, is having an affair with Myrtle, a woman from the poverty-stricken Valley of the Ashes. Gatsby has dedicated the most recent years of his life trying to win back his former love, Daisy. Conflict arises as Daisy, married to hulking Tom Buchanan, tries to understand her feelings; Tom tries to juggle his wife and his mistress; and Nick tries to make sense of all he has been thrust into. Cheating, lies, misunderstandings, and vengeance all ensue under a backdrop of obvious symbolism, and though it is the era of Prohibition, alcohol runs freely, people drive recklessly, and lives are ruined. Multiple themes connected to wealth, dreams, and disillusionment are developed, and the reader is left to ponder existential questions regarding the pursuit of the American Dream and the connections between wealth and happiness.

We Were Liars by E. Lockhart

E. Lockart's (2014) *We Were Liars* gives readers a glimpse at modern-day wealth and, like *The Great Gatsby*, the corruption that can be connected to having excess. The novel centers on the Sinclair family, and the summers they spend together on Beechwood Island in Massachusetts. Harris Sinclair, the patriarch of the family, has hoarded his wealth and pitted his children against one another in their pursuance of a large inheritance. Protagonist Cadence (Cady) Sinclair is the oldest grandchild and has spent every summer on the island with her cousins, collectively known as "The Liars." In some ways, the novel is a typical reminiscence of summer romances, full of teen parties, friendships, family drama, and first love.

However, the structure of the book is not linear, and while vicariously experiencing the Liars' summer fun, the reader must try to decipher not only the plot of the story but also whether Cady as a narrator is reliable in sharing the events that have transpired. Cady has experienced some sort of trauma during her 15th summer on the island, and she is not only unable to remember any of the events that have happened, but she also suffers from terrible headaches in the years following summer fifteen. The novel is almost a mystery, with Cady, with the help of the Liars, trying to put the pieces of her past together and to heal from the devastating losses she has experienced. Like *The Great Gatsby*, alcohol also runs freely, people are reckless, and lives are ruined in *We Were Liars*, and similar themes connected to wealth, health, and disillusionment are developed. Also like *The Great Gatsby*, *We Were Liars* leaves the reader wondering whether or not money really can buy happiness, and if trauma and addiction discriminates between the haves and the have-nots.

BEFORE READING

Exploring Substance Abuse Statistics and Resources

According to a national survey funded by the National Institute on Drug Abuse (2020) 38 percent of 12th graders indicated that they used an illegal substance in 2019. Alcohol use is even more prevalent among young adults with 19.3 percent of 8th graders, 37.7 percent of 10th graders, and 52.1 percent of 12th graders, indicating that they consumed alcohol in 2019 (National Institute on Drug Abuse, 2020). Regarding abuse of prescription (Rx) opioid pain relievers, ADHD (attention deficit hyperactivity disorder) stimulants, and anti-anxiety medications, young adults are the biggest abusers, with 12 percent of 18–25-year-olds, 6 percent of 12–17-year-olds, and 5 percent of adults 25 and older having used prescription drugs nonmedically in 2016 (National Institute on Drug Abuse, 2016).

As these statistics demonstrate, it is likely that most students in secondary classrooms across the nation will have some sort of experience with substance abuse, be it their own personal challenges or those of family members and/ or friends. Therefore, when pairing and teaching *The Great Gatsby* and *We Were Liars* with a focus on substance abuse, teachers should first guide students in exploring basic information regarding substance abuse in the United States, using primary source websites like the Center for Disease Control and Prevention (2020), the National Institute on Drug Abuse (2020), the National Substance Abuse Center on Addiction (2020), and the Substance Abuse and Mental Health Services Administration (n.d.). Teachers might, for example, first have students take the 2019 National Drug and Alcohol IQ Challenge to test their knowledge. The quiz can be done on the computer, or pdf versions can be downloaded from the National Institute on Drug Abuse for Teens website (2020). Completing this quiz individually and checking their answers with those provided can help students evaluate their personal knowledge in a safe environment. Teachers might then lead students in discussing anything from the quiz that was surprising, unpacking stereotypes and misconceptions that emerge, as well as sharing any other relevant information.

Teachers might also share the warning signs of substance abuse with students, encouraging them to track these as they identify them in the novels they will be reading. A list, including signs like "changes in dress and grooming, sudden weight gain or loss, and loss of interest in usual activities or hobbies," can be found on the Center on Addiction (2017) website.

In addition, teachers should provide resources to students regarding how they can seek help for themselves or loved ones who might be struggling with substance abuse. The U.S. Department of Health and Human Services' Substance Abuse and Mental Health Services Administration (SAMHSA, n.

d.) website provides a variety of resources as well as the phone number for the National Helpline. However, school and community resources will most likely be even more useful for students to have at the ready. As an extension, teachers could have students do their own investigation of what resources and supports are available in their school and the surrounding community. If this information is not easily accessible, students might collect and consolidate the information they find, creating posters, a website, fliers, and so on and putting them in places where other students and community members can have easy access to the identified local supports.

Finally, the National Institute on Drug Abuse for Teens (NIDA for Teens) website (2020) has a variety of lesson plans teachers might want to incorporate into their pre-reading lessons. For example, there are curriculum plans with resources for teaching about the effects of substance use on the brain and learning, the dangers of mixing substances, and how to analyze messages and images in the media about drug use/abuse (NIDA Teens, 2020). In all cases, teachers should prepare students for the content they will be studying, making sure the classroom is a safe place to share ideas, not requiring students to participate in discussions if they do not volunteer, and always using affirming language when talking about those who struggle with substance abuse and addiction.

Prohibition

In addition to basic information about substance abuse, it will be important for teachers to provide background information about Prohibition prior to students reading *The Great Gatsby*. The excessive consumption of alcohol throughout the novel becomes even more problematic when students know that it was illegal to buy or sell at the time. To set the stage for learning and understanding, teachers might begin by asking the students how they would feel if they were told they could no longer drink coffee, energy drinks, or soda, that they can only drink water. Students can write or discuss how they would feel, the reason why those beverages might be being banned, what they would do to resist this new "law." These personal connections will help students to better understand how consumers felt during Prohibition. Teachers might follow this activity by showing students images of advertisements on Prohibition, having them pay close attention to how these ads connect drinking and morality through both words and images. Teachers might then have students watch clips from the Ken Burns and Lynn Novick documentary Prohibition, and after viewing, lead a class discussion on the meaning and impact of prohibition. As an extension, students can be teamed to complete an inquiry on other identified aspects of Prohibition and share their findings through a multimedia presentation. For example, a group might want to research the women of the prohibition movement or investigate the counties in the United States that are "dry," still don't permit the sale of alcohol.

DURING READING

After basic information regarding substance abuse is explored, teachers can guide students in analyzing the representations of substance abuse as presented in the companion texts *The Great Gatsby* and *We Were Liars*, focusing on the effects of the substance use on the plots, characters, and themes of the texts individually and then in comparison to one another.

Substance Abuse in *The Great Gatsby*

Consumption of alcohol is a regular part of *The Great Gatsby* despite the fact that it was illegal during the novel's Prohibition setting. Students can track the scenes where alcohol is present, speculating on the unwritten messages Fitzgerald might have been making about those who drink too much. For example, at the beginning of the novel, readers learn that narrator Nick Carraway is not a regular drinker. Upon his first visit to Tom and Daisy's house he explains, "Meanwhile Tom brought out a bottle of whiskey from a locked bureau door. I have been drunk just twice in my life and the second time was that afternoon, so everything that happened has a dim hazy cast over it although until after eight o'clock the apartment was full of cheerful sun" (p. 33). This scene sets up the rest of the book, where Nick and seemingly all with whom he is in contact are drinking copiously, yet no one seems to be having a particularly good time. From a literary analysis perspective, teachers can guide students in analyzing the effect of the words "dim hazy cast" juxtaposed to the "cheerful sun" and how the darkness may be foreshadowing events to come. This juxtaposition of opposites such as light and dark, happy and sad continues to be evident in the subsequent passages where alcohol is present.

During Gatsby's parties, many attendees are depicted in contradicting ways. A performer is described as having, "drunk a quantity of champagne and during the course of her song she had decided ineptly that everything was very very sad—she was not only singing, she was weeping, too" (p. 55). Another partygoer's disturbing behavior is explained: "'Oh she's all right now. When she's had five or six cocktails she always starts screaming like that'" (p. 113). These characters are clearly unhappy despite being at a party surrounded by opulent wealth, and alcohol seems to bring out their negative emotions and despair. Furthermore, in describing Daisy's wedding, Jordan Baker explains:

I came into her room half an hour before the bridal dinner and found her lying on her bed as lovely as the June night in her flowered dress—and as drunk as a monkey. She had a bottle of sauterne in one hand and a letter in the other. "Gratulate me," she muttered. "Never had a drink before but oh, how I do enjoy it."(p. 81)

Students can analyze passages referencing alcohol use like these, considering the effects of Fitzgerald's word choice and contradictions on the mood, tone, and theme development of the novel.

Overall, the majority of the characters in *The Great Gatsby* are, arguably, unlikeable and not respected. While this is not solely due to their use of illegal substances, messages are presented illuminating the fact that drinking is not something to be glamorized. When Jordan Baker is describing Daisy's past to Nick she says:

Daisy was popular in Chicago, as you know. They moved with a fast crowd, all of them young and rich and wild, but she came out with an absolutely perfect reputation. Perhaps because she doesn't drink. It's a great advantage not to drink among high-drinking people. You can hold your tongue and, moreover, you can time any little irregularity of your own so that everybody else is so blind that they don't see or care. (p. 82)

Teachers can guide students in analyzing their own opinions about the characters in general and this quote in particular, considering not just how they feel about the characters and why but also how the characters' consumption and indulgence contribute to students' opinions. Students can discuss why the characters drink and how the plot would be different if alcohol was not a part of it. Moreover, they can analyze what messages Fitzgerald might be making about substance abuse throughout the text and, looking to Fitzgerald's personal life, speculate why.

Substance Abuse in *We Were Liars*

As in *The Great Gatsby*, substance abuse is seamlessly woven into the plot of *We Were Liars*, providing another opportunity for students to track the scenes where alcohol is present, considering the unwritten messages Lockhart might be making about those who drink too much. Like *The Great Gatsby*, in *We Were Liars*, scenes where alcohol is involved are often described with contradictions and very strong, negative emotions. For example, after hearing that her love interest, Gat, has a girlfriend, protagonist Cady, "cried and bit my fingers and drank wine I snuck from the Clairmont pantry. I spun violently into the sky, raging and banging stars from their moorings, swirling and vomiting" (p. 16). Similarly, later, when speaking of the Liars, Cady explains, "We were a bit drunk. We'd been at the aunties' leftover wine since they left the island. The alcohol made me feel giddy and powerful until I stood in the kitchen alone. Then I felt dizzy and nauseated. . . . The wine was muddling my head now. I wasn't used to it" (p. 204). These contrasting images, of the stars and vomiting, of giddiness and nauseousness, are powerful to contemplate when analyzing the representations of underage drinking in the novel.

It isn't just the Liars' underage drinking that is depicted negatively, it is the adults' excessive alcohol consumption as well. Cady shares her disgust with the adults on the island, a disgust that ultimately results in tragedy. She explains:

> The aunties got drunk, night after night . . . and angrier, every time. Screaming at each other. Staggering around the lawn . . . We watched them quarrel over Gran's things and the art that hung in Clairmont—but real estate and money most of all. (p. 154)

Further, the aunties are described as "They drink a fuckload. They're getting drunk until the tears roll down their faces" (p. 183).

Arguably, alcohol abuse from both the adults and the teens in *We Were Liars* plays a part in the tragedy of summer fifteen, and teachers can guide students in analyzing what the role of alcohol was in the fire, the subsequent lives lost, and whether the traumatic events would have played out differently if the entire Sinclair family had been sober that day. In doing so, teachers might refer students to passages like the above as well as this one, where Johnny and Gat explain that tragic night: "'When they left we drank the wine they'd left corked in the fridge . . . Four open bottles. And Gat was so angry . . . And yes, we were stupid drunk, and yes, we thought they'd rip the family apart and I would never come here again'" (pp. 177–78).

While alcohol use is so apparent that readers may easily identify how alcohol use and abuse impact the plot and characters of the book, perhaps less obvious is Cadence's addiction to painkillers. Throughout the novel, Cady's frequent use of prescription pills is mentioned; however, many students may not immediately recognize that she is, as author Lockhart describes, "my opiate-addicted heiress heroine" (Lockhart, 2014, Authors note, p. 3). On the very first page of the novel, the Sinclair family is described as "athletic, tall, and handsome . . . old-money Democrats . . . It doesn't matter if trust-fund money in running out; if credit card bills go unpaid on the kitchen counter. It doesn't matter if there's a cluster of pill bottles on the bedside table" (p. 3), and throughout the novel it is apparent that appearances are of the utmost importance to the family. Cady's mother is constantly reprimanding her behavior and appearance, especially in conjunction with Cady expressing emotions. Her mother seems to be laser-focused on presenting perfection, largely in the hopes that this outward appearance will garner her a future inheritance. Teachers might guide students in examining if and how Cady's mother may be enabling Cady's drug use or perhaps ignoring it altogether through analysis of passages like this: "Mummy promises coffee to help me stay awake while the drugs are in my system. She says how long it's been since the aunts have seen me, how the littles are my cousins, too, after all. I have family obligations" (p. 77). Students might discuss how Cady does or does not fit in with stereotypes regarding those addicted to pills, contemplating from where those stereotypes come, and how they and other myths regarding substance abuse can be broken.

Furthermore, readers know that Cady is sick, and needs the medication, which makes it harder to identify her abuse of the pills. She explains,

> Welcome to my skull. A truck is rolling over the bones in my neck and head. The vertebrae break, the brains pop and ooze. A thousand flashlights shine in my eyes. The world tilts. I throw up. I black out. This happens all the time. . . . The pain started six weeks after my accident. Nobody was certain whether the two were related, but there was no denying the vomiting and weight loss and general horror. Mummy took me for MRIs and CT scans. Needles, machines. More needles, more machines. They tested me for brain tumors, meningitis, you name it. To relieve the pain they prescribed this drug and that drug and another drug, because the first one didn't work and the second one didn't work, either. They gave me prescription after prescription without even knowing what was wrong. Just trying to quell the pain. Cadence, said the doctors, don't take too much. Cadence, said the doctors, watch for signs of addiction. And still, Cadence, be sure to take your meds. There were so many appointments I can't even remember them. Eventually the doctors came through with a diagnosis. Cadence Sinclair Eastman: post-traumatic headaches, also known as PTHA. Migraine headaches caused by traumatic brain injury. (pp. 33–34)

Students might research opioid addiction and debate the ethical obligations of pharmaceutical companies and doctors when prescribing these pain relievers to patients. They might refer back to the warning signs they learned about before reading these companion novels, and trace those that are evident in Cady. For example, she explains, "the year after my accident, I missed days and even weeks of school. I failed my classes, and the principal informed me I would have to repeat junior year. I stopped soccer and tennis. I couldn't babysit. I couldn't drive. The friends I'd had weakened into acquaintances" (p. 36). She is further described as "the sickly daughter [who] doesn't talk much. People who know her at school tend to keep away. They didn't know her well before she got sick anyway. She was quiet even then. Now she misses school half the time. When she's there, her pale skin and watery eyes make her look glamorously tragic, like a literary heroine wasting from consumption. Sometimes she falls down at school, crying. She frightens the other students. Even the kindest ones are tired of walking her to the nurse's office" (pp. 38–39).

It seems that Cady's youngest cousin, Taft, is the only one who recognizes Cady's problem and confronts her about it.

"Is it true you're a drug addict?" Taft asks me.
"No."
"Are you sure?"
"You're calling to ask if I'm a drug addict?" . . .
"Are you sure you're not a drug addict?"
"Where did you even get that idea?"
"Connie. She says I should watch out for you . . . I wanted to call you. Only not
    if you are a drug addict because drug addicts don't know what's going on."
"I'm not a drug addict, you pipsqueak," I say. Though
    possibly I am lying. (pp. 57–58)

Later, Taft brings up the issue again:

"Cady?" Taft touches my shoulder. "Bonnie saw pills in your bedroom . . . You told me you weren't a drug addict, but you have pills on your dresser . . . If you're a drug addict, says Taft, there is something you need to know." "What?" "Drugs are not your friend." Taft looks serious. Drugs are not your friend and also people should be your friends. (p. 92)

Teachers can guide students in analyzing the effect of having the youngest Sinclair being the only one to notice and ask Cady about her drug use and what that means to Cady and to readers' opinions of the other characters in the book. They can discuss whether or not they think Cady realizes she has a problem, and why she has not yet sought help. Finally, comparisons can be made to *The Great Gatsby* and the eyes of Dr. T. J. Eckleburg, watching over the corruption, seemingly the only thing to see the truth of what is happening, with a focus on the literary techniques that contribute to this shared plot point.

Cady's drug addiction and her feelings about herself and her situation offer opportunities for teachers to bring in mental health experts or to guide students in researching aspects of mental and emotional wellbeing. In particular, teachers might guide students in exploring how all feelings are valid, and how they should not feel guilty or embarrassed if they are struggling with their mental wellness, including substance abuse. Cady shares:

I know no one's beating me . . . I know I have plenty of money and a good education. Food on the table. I'm not dying of cancer. Lots of people have it much
worse than I . . . I shouldn't complain or be ungrateful . . . But listen. You have
no idea what it feels like to have headaches like this . . . It makes it hard to be
alive, some days. A lot of times I wish I were dead, I truly do, just to make the
pain stop . . . I just want the pain to be over . . . On the days the pills don't work.
I want it to end and I would do anything-really, anything-if I knew for sure it
would end the pain. (p. 129)

Often young adults feel that their problems are insignificant when there are
other, larger problems in the world. However, feeling guilty about feeling bad
is unhealthy and can result in even more negative and destructive behavior.
Teachers can help students to unpack this concept regarding delegitimizing
personal challenges when there are other, perhaps larger, problems in the
world, and help them to identify coping mechanisms and supports to address
mental and emotional health challenges they may be facing.

Unreliable Narrators

Both *The Great Gatsby* and *We Were Liars* arguably have unreliable narrators, and substance use and abuse contribute to this unreliability. While Cady
has amnesia, and her constant use of prescription medications has altered her
memory and understanding of people and the world around her (e.g., "It's
nice to hear him say that. I wish I weren't so high," p. 136), Nick Carraway's
unreliability is more subtle. Chronological inconsistencies in his narration
have led some scholars to feel he is an unreliable narrator (Fitzgerald, 1925,
p. 193), not to mention that he drinks a great deal, which could also skew both
his memory and his perception of events. Moreover, a queer reading of *The
Great Gatsby* can lead students to analyzing the possibility that Nick is gay
or bisexual (Herman, 2017) and that his trying to hide his sexuality from his
friends and cousin contribute to his unreliability as a narrator.

Like Nick, Cady is struggling with how she fits in with her family, with her
friends, with her boyfriend, and with her familial legacy as an heir. It is probable that she turns to abuse of opioids in attempts to forget about the trauma
that she has partially caused, her guilt driving her amnesia, exacerbated by
the painkillers she uses. Teachers can guide students in examining the literary
technique of the unreliable narrator. For example, students can analyze the
structure of the plots in conjunction to the unreliable narrators and analyze
the effects of this literary technique on the reader's understanding and enjoy-
ment of the texts. Nick Carraway tells Gatsby's story as an outsider piecing it
together and filling in the blanks with his own opinions. Similarly, Cadence
Sinclair tells her own story, but it also is in pieces, as she tries to remember

the events of her past. Students can consider how each novel would change if a different narrator, or even an omniscient narrator revealed the plots, perhaps even rewriting excerpts of each book from different points of view and considering the effects of the change in narration on the books as a whole.

AFTER READING

Mottos

There are a variety of ways in which students can further compare and analyze both texts after completing their reading. An exploration of mottos both for personal use and in public service announcements is one way teachers can help students to connect the two texts, while relating to current events and the modern day.

In *We Were Liars*, Mirren says, "'I like the idea of a motto . . . I think an inspirational quote can get you through hard times'" (p. 101). She shares her own personal motto, "Be a little kinder than you have to" (p. 101), and the other Liars then share their personal mottos as well (e.g., "Do not accept an evil you can change" [p. 101]. "Always do what you are afraid to do" [p. 102]). Students can discuss what makes a motto powerful and inspiring to an individual. Then, students can create original mottos for various characters in *The Great Gatsby* as well as for themselves. They can share their motto with the class via a poster or multimedia presentation or use their motto as a component of personal narrative writing or community action.

Exploring Other Themes

The Great Gatsby and *We Were Liars* share multiple themes and existential questions. *Can wealth buy happiness? Is the pursuit of a dream more satisfying than the attainment of a dream? If something is only real to one individual, does that mean it is not real at all? How can appearances mask realities? Is it possible to have multiple "selves," and if so, what self should we show to the world?* These are among the many prompts that students can consider, via discussion and/or written reflection and essay writing while they are reading, drawing connections between not only the two novels but also history and the real world.

Wealth

Wealth is a theme that is largely developed in multiple ways throughout each novel. In fact, wealth serves as almost a character in each text, driving themes and lessons for the reader to investigate. The question of whether or not money leads to corruption can be debated. For example, Granddad in *We Were Liars* rants, "'This is the United States of America . . . In America, here is how we operate: We work for what we want, and we get ahead. We never take no for an answer, and we deserve the rewards of our perseverance" (p. 176). Students can compare Gatsby and Harris's quest for the American Dream. *Is the American Dream possible? Has the American Dream changed over time?* They can identify what both characters have, but then also identify what they do *not* have. They can brainstorm what their own personal American Dream is. Students can then further explore the idea of money leading to corruption, citing examples from history and modern-day events to support the stance they have taken on this idea.

Indeed, the characters themselves seem to be almost physical representations of wealth. For example, Gatsby describes Daisy in saying:

> "Her voice is full of money," . . . That was it. I'd never understood it before. It was full of money—that was the inexhaustible charm that rose and fell in it, the jingle of it, the cymbal's song of it . . . High in a white palace the king's daughter, the golden girl . . . . (p. 127)

Through Cady's fairy tales, readers can also see her family as the "king's daughter(s)" and "golden girls." Students can discuss questions like, *In what ways are the women characters in both texts "golden"? What are the benefits and drawbacks of being a "golden girl"?* Indeed, while it seems almost a universal desire to be a princess, a golden girl, and able to buy whatever you want, the "golden" women characters in both texts seem miserably unhappy.

However, it's not just the women characters who do not seem to be living a life full of joy. In *We Were Liars*, Johnny describes how, despite their wealth, the Sinclair family is greedy, unsatisfied, and always wanting more and more. He reflects:

> The aunties got drunk, night after night . . . And angrier, every time. Screaming at each other. Staggering around the lawn . . . We watched them quarrel over Gran's things and the art that hung in Clairmont—but real estate and money most of all. Granddad was drunk on his own power and my mother wanted me to make a play for the money. (p. 154)

Students can debate whether or not money can buy happiness, using the texts as well as other pieces of literature, film, and real life as examples to support their claims. Cady says to her mother:

> Some people have nothing. We have everything. The only person who used the family money for charity was Gran. Now she's gone and all anyone's worried

about is her pearls and her ornaments and her real estate. Nobody is trying to use their money for good. Nobody is trying to make the world any better. (p. 162)

Teachers can have students debate whether or not the wealthy have a responsibility to use their money for good and to make the world a better place, citing examples from history and current events. Questions like these can also be examined in writing, or discussed among classmates as they consider this shared theme.

What is real?

Another theme developed in both novels is whether or not the pursuit of a dream is more satisfying than the attainment of it, and whether or not illusion is better than reality. Gatsby spent years and years building his wealth, putting Daisy on a pedestal, and waiting to be reunited with her. It seems impossible that the real Daisy could ever meet the expectation of the illusion of her that Gatsby had created. Nick explains:

> For a while these reveries provided an outlet for his (Gatsby's) imagination; they were a satisfactory hint of the unreality of reality, a promise that the rock of the world was founded securely on a fairy's wing I saw that the expression of bewilderment had come back into Gatsby's face, as though a faint doubt had occurred to him as to the quality of his present happiness. . . . There must have been moments even that afternoon when Daisy tumbled short of his dreams— not through her own fault but because of the colossal vitality of his illusion. It had gone beyond her, beyond everything. He had thrown himself into it with a creative passion, adding to it all the time, decking it out with every bright feather that drifted his way. No amount of fire or freshness can challenge what a man will store up in his ghostly heart. (Fitzgerald, 1925, pp. 101–5)

Cady's reality is also often "unreal." Whether her loss and/or reinterpreting of reality is drug or trauma-induced, students can identify in what ways *her* reality is unreal. Moreover, in both novels, there is copious drinking, with characters often so drunk that they make terrible decisions that have tragic results, and Lockhart even describes her protagonist, Cady, as "my opiate-addicted heiress heroine" (Lockhart, 2014, Authors note, p. 3). Whether it is in relation to their use and abuse of, largely illegal for the time period and their ages, substances or because they want so badly to believe things that aren't true, Cady and Gatsby often distort reality. Students can analyze the effects of these distortions on other characters in the books as well as on the plot.

Furthermore, students can contemplate whether or not Cady is better off not remembering what happened. A close examination of the fairy tales Cady writes can also help students to make connections to this theme. Whether characters are on some level *choosing* to believe a reality that they want so desperately or creating an alternate reality through no conscious effort of all, students can discuss, *What makes something real?* Nick says, "It is invariably saddening to look through new eyes at things upon which you have expended your own powers of adjustment" (p. 111). Teachers might ask students *How can this idea of self-adjustment of reality connect to Cady in* We Were Liars*? Provide other examples from history, current events, your personal experiences.*

Repeating the Past

A final example of a shared theme is the question of whether or not it is possible to escape and/or repeat the past. Gatsby believes both are possible, and he says this directly as he explains his background to Nick:

> "After that I lived like a young rajah . . . trying to forget something very sad that had happened to me long ago" (p. 70). Then, "You see I usually find myself among strangers because I drift here and there trying to forget the sad thing that happened to me." (p. 72)

While Gatsby is trying to forget the "sad thing that happened" to him, Cady is trying to remember. Gatsby collects things; Cady gives her things away. In requesting he not ask too much of his cousin Daisy, Nick tells Gatsby, "'You can't repeat the past' to which Gatsby replies, 'Can't repeat the past? Why of course you can!'" Teachers might provide prompts to students such as *Is it possible to repeat the past? Why or why not? In what ways do Cady and the Liars try to repeat the past? Are they successful? How do you know? In looking back on history as well as in our own lives, in what ways have we as a society escaped the past? In what ways have we repeated it?*

EXTENSION ACTIVITIES

Personal and Widespread Mottos

As an extension of the creation of mottos in the after-reading section, teachers can move students forward in considering their own personal mottos. For example, one teacher in the Pacific Northwest who paired these two novels guided her students in using them as inspiration for creating a social action plan (Boyd, 2017; Boyd & Darragh, 2019a, 2019b) for their high school.

These 10th graders were very drawn to the idea of having a personal motto like the characters in *We Were Liars*. They chose Mirren and Cady's motto, "Be a little kinder," and developed a plan to engage their classmates in small acts of kindness for the remainder of the school year. The students made T-shirts with "Be a little kinder" printed on them, put up signs connected to kindness around the building, and created bulletin boards where students, faculty and staff could share when they had been the recipients of kindness from others in the school. Their awareness project was met with success, and the students were able to plan their next action—bringing kindness into their community.

Following an exploration of individual mottos, teachers can guide students in extending the activity by looking at widespread mottos, specifically those that target teens in conjunction with substance abuse public service announcements. For example, teachers might have students listen to the Boston NPR news station's (2018) six-minute segment "How anti-drug campaigns like 'This is your brain on drugs' did and didn't work,'" and/or read the article "The effectiveness of anti-drug campaigns" (Scottsdale, 2018). Teachers can then lead students in discussion and debate regarding ad campaigns in general, and ads targeting teens specifically, with a focus on antidrug messages. Students can analyze different current and past anti-drug campaigns from around the world, identifying the effectiveness and ineffectiveness of each. The Drug Aware (n.d.) website shares current and past campaigns in Australia, each focusing on a different topic such as "Meth can take control," "Drug Driving," and "78% don't use." Similarly, the Above the Influence website (n.d.) provides a quiz for students to take, blog posts on topics such as "Privilege Pressure and Pills" (2016) and links to YouTube videos of past and current antidrug campaigns. Students can then use what they have learned to create their own anti-substance abuse campaigns that can be shared in their school and/or communities.

Expressing the Effects of Substance Abuse through Art

Art is one powerful way to express the effects of substance abuse on individuals, families, and communities. Teachers can guide students in researching about other artists who are believed to have struggled with substance abuse like Frida Kahlo, Jackson Pollock, Pablo Picasso, Vincent Van Gogh, and Andy Warhol, helping them to analyze the artwork, looking for patterns and themes among pieces. Students can then create their own artwork to share messages regarding substance use, abuse, addiction, recovery, and/or hope, perhaps modeling after their chosen artist's style. They can create their own art show and/or display their work throughout the school and in their communities.

Alternatively, or in addition to a focus on painting and drawing, teachers might look to other forms of the arts for extension activities. For example, nearly every genre of music has songs connected to substance abuse. Teachers can help students to identify different songs that reference substance use and abuse, and to analyze not just the lyrics but also each song's tone, the era the song was composed, and the musical genre. The class as a whole can then track patterns uncovered, considering if representations of substance abuse are different in various genres (e.g., country versus rock and roll) as well as if depictions are different in the music of the 1900s versus the 2000s, and why that might be. Students can contemplate the target audience for different songs, and track how each song's music videos appeal to their intended audience. Further, they can research what was going on in the world during the time the song was released, how that could impact the writer and the consumer, and how those representations in songs compare to representations of substance abuse in art, film, and literature. Students might also identify music that does not have lyrics, but that they think captures the effects of substance abuse on individuals and families, rewrite lyrics of songs they like to include messages regarding substance abuse and recovery, and/or even compose their own music on this topic.

CONCLUSION

From issues of health, wealth, substance use and abuse, to themes of guilt, dreams, and disillusionment, pairing *The Great Gatsby* and *We Were Liars* offers teachers and students opportunities to think critically about how substance abuse can affect individuals, families, friends, and communities. Moreover, it allows students a safe environment to research about substance abuse, dispel stereotypes about those who struggle with addiction, and learn of ways to procure help for themselves and others in need.

REFERENCES

Above the influence. (n.d.). https://abovetheinfluence.com/.

Above the influence. (2016, September 15). Privilege pressure and pills. https://abovetheinfluence.com/privilege-pressure-pills/.

Addiction and art. (2010–2020). https://www.addictionandart.org/.

Boyd, A. S. (2017). *Social justice literacies in the English classroom.* New York: Teachers College Press.

Boyd, A. S., & Darragh, J. J. (2019a). Critical literacies on the university campus: Engaging pre-service teachers with social action projects. *English Teaching: Practice & Critique, 19*(1), 49–63.

Boyd, A. S., & Darragh, J. J. (2019b). *Reading for action: Engaging youth in social justice through young adult literature.* Lantham, MD: Rowman and Littlefield.

Center on Addiction. (2017). Teen substance use. https://www.centeronaddiction.org /addiction-prevention/teenage-addiction.

Centers for Disease Control and Prevention. (2020). National center for health statistics. https://www.cdc.gov/nchs/fastats/alcohol.htm.

Drug Aware. (n.d.). Current campaigns. https://drugaware.com.au/about-us/current -campaigns/.

Fitzgerald, F. S. (1925). *The great Gatsby.* Scribner.

Herman, D. (2017). *The great Gatsby's* Nick Carraway: His narration and his sexuality. *ANQ: A Quarterly Journal of Short Articles, Notes and Reviews, 30*(4), 247–50.

Lockhart, E. (2014). *We were liars.* Delacorte.

National Institute on Drug Abuse. (2016). Abuse of prescription drugs affects young adults the most. https://www.drugabuse.gov/related-topics/trends-statistics/infogr aphics/abuse-prescription-rx-drugs-affects-young-adults-most.

National Institute on Drug Abuse. National Institutes of Health. U.S. Department of Health and Human Services. (2020). https://www.drugabuse.gov/related-topics/ trends-statistics.

National Institute on Drug Abuse for Teens. (2020a). Stats and trends in teen drug use with interactive chart. https://teens.drugabuse.gov/teachers/stats-and-trends-t een-drug-use.

National Institute on Drug Abuse for Teens. (2020b). Teachers: Classroom resources on drug effects. https://teens.drugabuse.gov/teachers.

PBS. (2011). Prohibition in the classroom. https://www.pbs.org/kenburns/prohibition /educators/.

Scottsdale Recovery Center. (2018, October 23). The effectiveness of anti-drug campaigns. https://scottsdalerecovery.com/effectiveness-of-anti-drug-campaigns/.

Substance Abuse and Mental Health Services Administration. (n.d.). https://www .samhsa.gov/.

The National Substance Abuse Center on Addiction. (2020). https://www.centeron addiction.org/newsroom/press-releases/national-center-addiction-and-substance -abuse-releases-comprehensive-guide.

WBUR. (2018, May 29). How anti-drug campaigns like "This is your brain on drugs" have and haven't worked. https://www.wbur.org/hereandnow/2018/05/29/anti-dr ug-campaigns-effectiveness.

Chapter 5

Justice Served?

Teaching Native Son *and* Allegedly

Lisa Scherff

Richard Wright's *Native Son* and Tiffany Jackson's *Allegedly*, published nearly 80 years apart, make for a fitting pairing in secondary English classes: both novels feature protagonists of color who are charged with murder, do not have access to equitable educational opportunities, are raised by single mothers, and face an unfair and unjust judicial system.

While a demanding text, *Native Son* is one of my sophomore students' favorite novels of the year, one which challenges their beliefs and assumptions and leads to a fruitful discussion of prejudice in this country. However, not all schools teach this controversial and groundbreaking text. Moreover, given its distance, historically, to many of today's students, it can require much frontloading of information (e.g., time period, politics, racism, Wright's background).

Because of these reasons, providing a scaffold or text-to-text connection is critical for many students. I offer the young adult novel *Allegedly* as a complementary text for examining many of the issues and themes (e.g., blackness/whiteness, racism, fear can drive one to commit horrible acts, one's environment influences behavior) presented in Wright's classic. *Allegedly* is such an approachable yet complex text that teachers can offer Jackson's novel by itself or as a bridge to its canonical connection. The novel is an excellent pairing with *Native Son* because it too does not present events in black and white and raises questions about equity, the justice system, the notion of truth, and how easy it might be to cross a line.

I also argue that these two novels are important—but especially *Allegedly* as a preface to *Native Son*—because with multicultural texts, students might struggle with interpretation and/or inferential thinking because they are unfamiliar with the cultures presented in them, resulting in unwillingness to explore issues of race and White privilege (Beach et al., 2003).

Native Son by Richard Wright

Native Son (1940) by Richard Wright tells the story of 20-year-old Bigger Thomas, who, on his first night working as a driver for a wealthy White family, the Daltons, in Hyde Park, ends up killing their daughter, Mary. Set 1930s, African Americans like Bigger are caught in a cycle of poverty and lack of education, due to systemic racism through redlining, unfair housing prices, and prejudiced law enforcement and prosecutors. The rash murder Bigger commits is followed by a series of poor decisions—due in large part to Bigger knowing what the White system will say and/or even create stories of what happened rather than listen to why and how it happened—which leads to him being tried for and convicted of murder. The novel has long been a staple in upper-level English classes and on the Advanced Placement exam, being listed as an open-response title at least ten times.

Allegedly by Tiffany Jackson

Tiffany Jackson's *Allegedly* (2017) is the first-person account of Mary B. Addison, a Black teenager who spent six years in "baby jail" (i.e., in isolation in an adult prison) after being tried for and convicted of killing a three-month-old baby in her mother's care. Now, she is in a poorly run group home with other teenage girls who have been in trouble with the law. During her mandated community service at a nursing home, she meets Ted, a teenager also doing community service, and becomes pregnant. Wanting to keep her baby and go to college, Mary wants to set the record straight about what really happened that night all those years ago. Why she killed baby Alyssa, allegedly. The novel is an excellent pairing with *Native Son* because it too does not present easy answers to complex questions while also raising questions about the influence of adults in young people's lives, the juvenile justice system, what counts as the truth, and second chances for young offenders.

BEFORE READING

Before reading *Native Son*, class time should be devoted to a discussion of the n-word in Wright's novel and learning about key topics related to the time the novel was written.

The *N*-Word

One pre-reading lesson is centered on the use of the *n*-word as Wright does not hold back in his portrayal of the time, and how people of color were referred to by many racist citizens. Use of the *n*-word is a hotly contested issue not only in society but also in classrooms, with teachers themselves debating whether the word should be read aloud when it is in a text. As Dave Sheinin and Krissah Thompson (2014) noted in their *Washington Post* article, there is no other word in the English language that embodies both the ugliest hate and a shared, subversive sense of love and regard, depending upon who is saying it and in what context.

Students begin by reading and responding to Sheinin and Thompson's article; this could be accomplished through a combination of methods (homework reading, think-pair-share, journaling, student-raised questions, and/or discussion, etc.). Then, have students view short video excerpt from a Q&A panel with Ta-Nehisi Coates (Random House, 2017) where he addresses a young White woman's question about whether it is acceptable to use the *n*-word. In this video, using analogies with words like "honey," "bitch," and "faggot," Coates explains that people within the groups or communities using these words with each other are different than outsiders employing them towards members of those groups. Turning to the *n*-word itself, Coates asserts that Whites are "taught that everything belongs to you. You think you have a right to everything." Thus, some Whites are upset and feel it is "racist" that they cannot use the word they hear (in rap songs, for example). Coates' final point is that this experience—of not using a word—is a small example of what it is like to be Black in this country.

After watching the short video, have students answer three questions on their own: *What is the main point that Ta-Nehisi Coates is making in the video? What did he say that makes you think that? What do you think about his argument(s)?* After students respond to the questions, a class discussion can be held either with partners first then a whole class or as a whole-class conversation. This type of class discussion can very helpful and enlightening for students.

Redlining

To try to fully understand who Bigger Thomas is and why he acted as he did, students need a great deal of background knowledge on Richard Wright and the time period (1930s) and setting (Chicago) of the novel. Indeed, the concept of "institutional forces" (i.e., the effects of race and class) is critical. Topics such as redlining, racism, the first Red Scare, the Great Migration, the Scottsboro Boys, Marxism, and naturalism provide students with a solid foundation for reading the novel.

Here, the focus is on redlining because in my experience it has been one of the most impactful concept for students, one they mentioned throughout the year (it carried into our reading of *The Great Gatsby*, for example). What is redlining? According to the Fair Housing Act (2006), redlining is the custom of denying a creditworthy applicant a home loan in a particular area even though the candidate may otherwise be eligible. This practice goes back nearly 90 years.

The government-sponsored Home Owners' Loan Corporation (HOLC) and the Federal Housing Administration were created in the 1930s to help Americans keep and refinance their homes. However, these organizations explicitly provided housing opportunities for White homeowners while denying and segregating Blacks through redlining: refusing to insure mortgages in and near African American neighborhoods (Gross, 2017). These decisions were presented through maps drawn for major cities across the country with areas shaded from green to red.

As reported on the website Mapping Inequality, a collaboration among researchers from several universities, HOLC staff used data prepared by real estate stakeholders (e.g., lenders, developers, appraisers) in each city to assign grades to residential neighborhoods that reflected their "mortgage security" that were then envisioned on color-coded maps. Communities that received a grade of A (green on the maps) were considered minimal risks for banks and mortgage lenders when they were deciding who should get loans and which areas were secure investments. Those receiving the lowest grade of D, shaded red, were considered "hazardous."

A 1937 appraisal manual outlined the grade descriptions:

- Grade A = "homogeneous," in demand during "good times or bad."
- Grade B = "like a 1935 automobile-still good, but not what the people are buying today who can afford a new one."
- Grade C = becoming obsolete, "expiring restrictions or lack of them" and "infiltration of a lower grade population."
- Grade D = "those neighborhoods in which the things that are now taking place in the C neighborhoods, have already happened."

(cited in Aaronson, Hartley, & Mazumder, 2019, p. 7)

These grade descriptions were tools for redlining and made it challenging or impossible for people in certain neighborhoods to become homeowners. Redlining directed both public and private money to native-born Whites and away from African Americans and immigrants. As homeownership was perhaps the most important method of "intergenerational wealth building in the United States in the twentieth century, these redlining practices from eight decades ago had long-term effects in creating wealth inequalities that we still see today" (Mapping Inequality).

Students should understand the devastating effects of redlining in Chicago in order to understand Bigger Thomas and his family. They are stuck in a cycle of poverty due to the overpriced rent charged by White slumlords in the area of town in which they—and most other Blacks—are segregated (ironically, it is the White benefactor, Mr. Dalton, who has invested in the company that owns their building). It is crucial to show maps of the city from the time, identifying Bigger's neighborhood and Hyde Park, where the Daltons live. The maps can be used as a reference, especially in Books 1–2 of the novel. Mapping Inequality's Redlining Inequality in New Deal America offers interactive maps that students can explore.

DURING READING

Students' pre-reading work related to redlining, connects with during-reading analysis that utilizes Marxism and naturalism because redlining is inherently tied to issues of power and class (Marxism). And, redlining creates specific environments for people to live in, which is tied to a naturalistic style of writing for *Native Son* and *Allegedly*. While reading the novels one strategy works particularly well, theory/literary style tracing. When tracing a theory throughout a novel, students should have a theory guide to help them identify aspects of the texts that fit or relate to it.

Marxist Theory and Analysis

What is Marxist criticism? In short, Marxism relates to power and class and how those are represented in a text. In a Marxist reading of a text, the reader seeks to answer any of the following kinds of questions (modified from Delahoyde, n.d.): *What role does social class play in the work? How does the author present class relations?*

In *Native Son*, for example, class—which is directly tied to race—is foundational not only to the plot but also as motivation for Richard Wright in authoring the novel. As he wrote of his character Bigger in the Introduction, "he is a dispossessed and disinherited man . . . he lives amid the greatest possible plenty on earth (p. xx) . . . hovering unwanted between two worlds—between powerful America and his own stunted place in life" (p. xxiv).

Bigger, his two siblings, and his mother live in a run-down, one-room apartment with a rent of $8 per week (approximately $125 today). When the novel opens, the family is scrambling frantically to kill a huge rat that is tormenting them again. Bigger reflects on how "the shame and misery of their lives [would sweep him] out of himself with fear and despair" (p. 13). That scene stands in stark contrast to where the Dalton family lives, a "quiet and spacious white neighborhood" (p. 45), where he is offered $25 a week to be the family's driver.

How do characters overcome oppression?

In *Allegedly*, the main way Mary tries to overcome systemic oppression is to take the SAT and earn a good score enough so she can go to college. During her time in jail, despite stating her college goals, Mary was dissuaded from this by the adults she encountered and told instead she should think about cosmetology as a career.

In what ways does the novel try to disrupt the status quo?

Native Son, in its entirety, disrupts the status quo. As discussed by John Reilly in the Afterword, the novel reverses the typical story of the Black man as "pitiable" by making him the "violent attacker" (p. 393). Yet, Bigger's realizations about this violence ironically lead him to a sort of freedom at the end. In a similar fashion, *Allegedly*—as a whole—disrupts notions of Black and White when it comes to children and crime and the truth. Did Mary do it? If she did, was it accidental or purposeful? Is she really on a path to be a good mother? To further discussion on this topic, as students to consider what the novel says about oppression.

Are the social conflicts ignored or blamed elsewhere?

Oppression and social conflicts are front and center in *Native Son*, and Wright makes it clear that the White tyranny and racism are to blame for Black citizens' problems. Early in the novel, when Bigger and his friend Gus are walking down the street, Bigger asks Gus, "You know where the white folks live?" (p. 24). When Gus provides a literal, geographic answer, Bigger punches his own stomach and replies, "Right down here in my stomach" (p. 24), indicating how the Whites live and what opportunities they have almost fester inside of him.

Does the novel propose some form of utopian vision as
a solution to the problems shown in the work?

The only characters in *Native Son* that seem to provide any utopian vision are those that belong to the Communist party—Jan, Mary's boyfriend, and Max, the lawyer who tries to save Bigger. The inclusion of these characters is interesting to the story as a whole because Bigger, based on his experience with White people, distrusts them. And, in fact, it is Bigger's distrust of Jan that somewhat sets him down the path to kill Mary. Jan's notions of revolution, with Blacks and Whites being equal with "no rich and no poor" (p. 69), make Bigger very uneasy. His first encounter with Mary and Jan made him feel "things he did not want to feel" (p. 69); "he did not understand them; he distrusted them, really hated them" (p. 71).

One way to read the novel(s) is to keep a reading journal using the Marxist lens (and/or questions) with text evidence in one column and analysis/explanation in the other. For example, because of their race, class, and lack of education, both Bigger and Mary are distrustful of others who are different. In Bigger's case, he cannot comprehend why two White people—one a Communist (Jan) and the other a wealthy college girl (Mary Dalton)—talk to him like he is one of them or why they want him to sit with them to grab a quick dinner at a diner, things outside the realm of his life experiences as a Black man. These interactions make him uneasy and angry and, ultimately, lead to him killing Mary. In *Allegedly*, Mary Addison also faces others who she distrusts because of her history with the judicial system and adults in general. However, unlike Bigger, some of these adults she decides to trust, and her outcome is different from his (see figure 5.1)

Naturalism

Another way to read and respond is by tracing elements that make the novel a naturalistic text. A naturalistic novel shows a graphic account, often a narrative of despair. As such, studying naturalism before reading *Native Son* and/or *Allegedly* is recommended, especially for Wright's novel as it fits this genre.

Naturalism in literature is an emphasis on how heredity, environment, and surroundings affect a character (conflicts of man vs. man and/or man vs. nature). Incorporating naturalism as a lens while reading is also a valuable practice because it can be used as a framework, or purpose, for reading. As many students struggle with comprehension, having a purpose for reading is critical.

Text Evidence	Analysis
NS: "We'll own all that some day, Bigger," Jan said with a wave of his hand. "After the revolution it'll be ours. But we'll have to fight for it. What a world to win, Bigger! And when that day comes, things'll be different. There'll be no white and no black; there'll be no rich and no poor" . . . These people made him feel things he did not want to feel. If he were white, if he were like them, it would have been different. But he was black. (p. 69)	Jan is part of the Communist party, and the things he is telling Bigger--and how he is talking to Bigger--make Bigger uncomfortable not only because in his world white men do not interact with Black me this way but also because he is scared of the repercussions of being around a "Red."
A: "Listen to me, 'ere chile, don't ever let anyone stop yuh from bettering yourself. Yuh scared of people knowing yuh scared of change? Good. Change is scary. Get used to it! But nothing comes from nothing" . . . My head drops like it always does when I'm being lectured . . . [she] makes me feel stupid. (pp. 82-83)	Mary has been used to the adults in her life letting her down, exerting power over her that she does not understand. When Mary is encouraged to get help for and take the SAT, she is hesitant and distrustful of this woman who seems to really care. Like Bigger, the situation makes her feel stupid and uneasy.

Figure 5.1 Sample Reading Journal. Created by author.

Several common themes can be found in naturalistic novels, and any or all of these can be traced and discussed during reading (Walcutt, 1956):

- The "beast within" each individual, composed of powerful and often conflicting emotions (lust, greed, or the need for dominance or pleasure, the struggle for survival)
- How heredity and environment affect and burden individuals
- An unfeeling, deterministic universe (Is there free will?)

As students read *Native Son*, ask them to look for instances where Bigger's background and environment seem particularly influential. Reading with naturalism in mind can also lead to comparing and contrasting the main characters, Bigger and Mary. Characters in naturalistic novels are often poorly educated or from the lower class; their lives are ruled by factors such as genetics, instinct, and/or suffering. Likewise, their efforts to exercise free will are crippled by external forces beyond their control, and this is often emphasized by having stories in urban settings (Campbell, 2017).

AFTER READING

Both novels, alone or together, offer work well with a range of after-reading strategies. One that works particularly well is using the concept of mens rea to analyze Bigger and Mary's crimes. *Mens rea* is the legal term used to describe the mental state a person must be in while committing a crime for it to be considered intentional (i.e., a general aim to break the law or a specified, premeditated plan). Mental states are generally organized by the offender's state of "blameworthiness." The blameworthiness of the accused's mental state correlates with the gravity of the crime. Higher levels of blameworthiness equate with more severe culpability and tougher sentencing. In other words, "a crime committed purposefully would carry a more severe punishment than if the offender acted knowingly, recklessly, or negligently" (Cornell Law School, n.d.). There are four levels of culpability when considering mens rea (listed from most to least culpability):

1. Intent (acting purposely): The defendant had an underlying conscious object to act.
2. Knowledge (acting knowingly): The defendant is practically certain that the conduct will cause a particular result.
3. Recklessness (acting recklessly): The defendant consciously disregarded a substantial and unjustified risk.

Bigger Thomas	Native Son	
Levels of Culpability	*Example from Book*	*Analysis/Explanation*
Intent	He did not purposely plan to kill Mary Dalton, and it wasn't impulse to murder her either. However, Bessie's murder is different. That was planned.	Bigger knew, as a Black man, that even being in Mary's room would be the charge of rape by White men. In his world, there was no cry of "I didn't do it."
Knowledge	Bigger was trying to keep Mary quiet, not purposely strangle her. So, he didn't know that he would kill her. With Bessie, Bigger knew bashing her head in would kill her	This repeats the row above. He believes that if Mr. Dalton even saw him in her room, he would get fired, and he needs the job. Because Mary was so drunk she could not stand up, Bigger felt an obligation to get her to her room safely. He was stuck no matter what.
Recklessness	It was reckless to hold his hand over Mary's mouth. He was intoxicated like she was, however. However, there was an equal risk in not trying to keep her quiet. He knew what he was doing when murdering Bessie; he even took her to an abandoned building to do so.	This also repeats the row above and is further supported by evidence later in the novel. Bigger is falsely accused of, and in the White people's eyes guilty of, raping other White women simply because he is Black. With Bessie's murder, it is almost as if Bigger did not give her any consideration or consider her murder as reckless at all; she was a liability because she knew of his plans.
Negligence	Bigger was negligent in killing Mary Dalton; he should have known that covering her mouth might hurt or kill her. This is hard to apply to Bessie's murder as it was a planned and conscious act.	As he did not set out to murder Mary, one could argue he should have been aware he could accidentally kill her. However, he was scared and intoxicated.

Figure 5.2 **Exploring Levels of Culpability in *Native Son*.** Created by author.

4. Negligence (acting negligently): The defendant was not aware of the risk but should have been aware of the risk.

To be convicted, "a criminal prosecutor must show beyond any reasonable doubt that the suspect actively and knowingly participated in a crime that harmed another person" (Mens Rea, 2017). Mens rea is often applied to murder cases; did the accused commit murder on purpose or accidentally? This question can be applied to both Bigger and Mary. After reading, students can work to fill in a chart for each or both of the novels (see figure 5.2). While the analysis for *Native Son* is rather straightforward, the same cannot be said for *Allegedly*, which is why it will be an interesting task for students. (See figure 5.3).

EXTENSION ACTIVITIES

Researching the Justice System

Both novels feature protagonists who did not receive equitable chances for an education. As extension activities, students could conduct research on the school-to-prison pipeline, the juvenile justice system (including trying and

Mary Addison	Allegedly	
Levels of Culpability	*Example from Book*	*Analysis/Explanation*
Intent	Throughout most of the novel, Mary is believed to have killed baby Alyssa. However, who really did? Mary or her mother? And, was there intent to do so?	Towards the end, Mary gives conflicting accounts with different levels of intent: "I gave her my pills" (p. 383); "I didn't mean to throw her!" (p. 383); "doing anything to get away from Momma. Even killing a baby" (p. 384). Can a nine-year-old have intent?
Knowledge	Alyssa had bruising on her forearms, upper right thigh, and center forehead, as well as on her face (p. 53); the cause of death was strangulation (p. 54)	If the mother killed the baby, then as an adult (and a nurse) she would know what type of actions cause death. If a nine-year-old kills a baby, is that the same? Also, if Mary's revelation that Ray and her mother beat her and had her on mood and ADHD drugs, then how might that have impacted and altered her brain at such a young age?
Recklessness	If the mother was responsible, then she disregarded a substantial and unjustified risk. If Mary killed Alyssa, how much does this apply?	Mary tells the girls at the group home several different versions of the truth: "I didn't mean to" (p. 373), "I didn't do it" (p. 375), and "it was an accident" (p. 373).
Negligence	Should Mary's mother have been aware of the risk? What about Mary?	If Mary gave her pills to Alyssa, she was only doing what her own mother and Ray gave to her. If the adults in her life told Mary that the pills were to shut her up, then in her mind, why not give them to a crying baby? During their last argument, Mary lets her mother know a fact she had not disclosed until then: "I didn't kill Ray but I know your pills sure did" (p. 369), indicating her mother is capable of murder.

Figure 5.3   **Exploring Levels of Culpability in *Allegedly*.** Created by author.

sentencing minors as adults), or prison reform, looking into programs like the Bard Prison Initiative, Shakespeare Behind Bars, and programs at San Quentin like the sports teams (e.g., San Quentin Giants baseball, San Quentin Warriors basketball), the annual marathon, and podcast (Ear Hustle). There have been several documentaries featuring these initiatives, which provide an avenue for critical media study as well. Students could create short videos on their topic and present to the whole class.

Exploring Other Young Adult Texts

Teachers could further the work with literature circles that feature fiction and nonfiction titles that include protagonists in the juvenile and/or adult prison systems, such as *Hole in My Life* by Jack Gantos, *We Were Here* by Matt de la Pena, *Monster* by Walter Dean Myers, *Always Running* by Luis J. Rodriguez, *Citizen Outlaw* by Charles Barber, or *Writing My Wrongs* by Shaka Senghor.

Writing about *Native Son* Using Past AP Prompts

To provide students with more options for writing, teachers could pull from past AP Literature Exam prompts that specifically mention *Native Son* and modify them to use as a summative assessment. For example,

- **1979.** Consider how Bigger or Mary, on the basis of their actions alone, might be considered evil or immoral. In a well-organized essay, explain both *how* and *why* the full presentation of the character in the novel makes us react more sympathetically than we otherwise might.
- **2001.** One definition of madness is "mental delusion or the eccentric behavior arising from it." Think about how in *Native Son* or *Allegedly* a character's seeming madness or irrational behavior plays an important role. Then write a well-organized essay in which you explain what this delusion or strange behavior consists of and how it might be judged reasonable. Explain the significance of the "madness" to the book as a whole.
- **2011.** In a novel by William Styron, a father tells his son that life "is a search for justice." Choose a character from the novel who responds in some significant way to justice or injustice. Then write a well-developed essay in which you analyze the (1) character's understanding of justice, (2) the degree to which the character's search for justice is successful, and (3) the significance of this search for the book as a whole.
- **2019.** Think about how in *Native Son* or *Allegedly* a character holds an "ideal view of the world." Then write an essay in which you analyze the character's idealism and its positive or negative consequences. Explain how the author's portrayal of this idealism highlights a theme of the book as a whole.

CONCLUSION

Through the pairing and studying of *Allegedly* and *Native Son*, students are provided an avenue for rich analysis and discussion surrounding many relevant topics, including but not limited to race, racism, and the justice system. Together, these texts raise questions about equity, justice, the notion of truth, and how easy it might be to cross a line, making their narratives a great place for students to explore these topics.

REFERENCES

Aaronson, D., Hartley, D., & Mazumder, B. (2019). *The effects of the 1930s HOLC "redlining" maps. WP 2017-12.* Federal Reserve Bank of Chicago.

Beach, R., Parks, D., Haertling Thein, A., & Lensmire, T. (2003). *High school students' responses to alternative stances associated with the study of multicultural literature.* Paper presented at the annual meeting of the American Educational Research Association, Chicago, IL. ED 477859.

Campbell, D. M. (2017). Naturalism in American literature. *Literary Movements.* Dept. of English, Washington State University. Retrieved from https://public.wsu .edu/~campbelld/amlit/natural.htm.

Cornell Law School. (n.d.). Mens Rea. Legal information institute. *Cornell Law School.* Retrieved from https://www.law.cornell.edu/wex/mens_rea.

Delahoyde, M. (n.d.). *Marxist criticism.* Retrieved from https://public.wsu.edu/~d elahoyd/marxist.crit.html.

Federal Reserve. (2006). Federal fair lending regulations and statutes fair housing act. *Consumer Compliance Handbook.* Retrieved from https://www.federalreserve.gov /boarddocs/supmanual/cch/fair_lend_fhact.pdf.

Gross, T. (2017). A "forgotten history" of how the U.S. government segregated America. *Fresh Air.* Retrieved from https://www.npr.org/2017/05/03/526655831/a -forgotten-history-of-how-the-u-s-government-segregated-america.

Jackson, T. (2017). *Allegedly.* New York, NY: Katherine Tegen Books.

Mapping Inequality. (n.d.). *Introduction.* Retrieved from https://dsl.richmond.edu/ panorama/redlining/#loc=4/37.76/-100.621&text=intro.

Mens Rea. (2017). *Crime museum.* Retrieved from https://www.crimemuseum.org/cr ime-library/criminal-law/mens-rea/.

Random House. (2017, November 17). *When every word doesn't belong to everyone* [Video]. YouTube. https://www.youtube.com/watch?v=QO15S3WC9pg.

Sheinin, D., & Thompson, K. (2014). Redefining the word: Examining a racial slur entrenched in American vernacular that is more prevalent than ever. *The Washington Post.* Retrieved from https://www.washingtonpost.com/sf/national /2014/11/09/the-n-word-an-entrenched-racial-slur-now-more-prevalent-than-ever/.

Walcutt, C. C. (1956). *American literary naturalism: A divided stream.* Westport, CT: Greenwood Press.

Wright, R. (2003). *Native son. Abridged edition: The original 1940 text.* New York, NY: Harper Perennial.

Chapter 6

They're Still Watching

1984, Little Brother, *and the Staying Power of the Techno-Dystopia*

Sarah Burriss and Melanie Hundley

Science fiction is more than escapist fiction. Noted science fiction writer Arthur C. Clarke argued that it is "a fiction which does concern itself with real issues: the origin of man; our future. In fact, [he couldn't] think of any form of literature which is more concerned with real issues, reality" ("Transhumanism and Post-Reality," n.d.). The challenge of teaching science fiction is how easily it is dismissed as not being real literature. The imagined worlds of science fiction have frequently served as predictors—or perhaps instigators—of different kinds of scientific and technological inventions.

Science fiction offers a kind of text that reimagines current and future worlds, much like a fortune teller's ball that provides a glimpse of a possible future. The very real issues that are explored in possible futures allow readers to think through, without actually having to experience, dystopian possibilities. It allows readers to imagine what happens if a computer takes over the world, or if a plague decimates a segment of the population, or if suddenly there is no more water. These texts may serve as cautionary tales or as opportunities to discuss current issues in a different context.

The novel *1984* is perhaps one of the most studied and referenced science fiction novels in recent memory, and it is easy to see its influence and relevance today. "Big brother" has become a recognizable trope in contemporary rhetoric. We can see the influence of Orwell's novel in popular culture ranging from TV reality shows like *Big Brother*, an international franchise where housemates are isolated and continuously surveilled by video and audio recording, to the "Make Orwell Fiction Again" tote bag available on the American Library Association's online store. The latter indicates that Orwell was so prescient in his novel that the fictional world of *1984* has become our reality.

Through direct references to this canonical work, *Little Brother* (Doctorow, 2008) does much of the heavy lifting in making visible the influence of Orwell's *1984* on contemporary popular culture. The eponymous "Little Brother" is the "sibling" of Orwell's "Big Brother," and the main character, w1n5t0n, is a clear reference to Orwell's Winston. Themes such as surveillance and privacy, technology and its role in society, media and how it shapes cultural narratives, and the role of protest and rebellion are pervasive in both texts, presenting many opportunities for comparison. In addition to providing an updated technological context, *Little Brother* adds an action-packed plot, young, more diverse protagonists, and a contemporary setting, including references to more current geopolitics.

In this chapter, we will show how *1984* and *Little Brother*, when taught thoughtfully in conjunction with one another, provide students with rich opportunities to think critically about our lives with technology and who gets to write which stories about them.

1984 by George Orwell

In *1984*, 39-year-old Winston lives in a dystopian, totalitarian world where the government, led by "Big Brother," establishes power over its citizens through a combination of surveillance, terror, and propaganda. Through its Ministries of Truth, Plenty, and Love—each of which in reality promotes the opposite of its name—the Party controls every aspect of Party members' lives. Their ultimate aim is not merely to instill fear but to control citizens' minds.

In Winston's Oceania, the world is at war and always has been. Winston works in the Ministry of Truth, where his job is to continually rewrite history based on the current whims and realities of the Party. Winston's dreary life changes when he illegally purchases and writes in a diary, an act of resistance that holds terrible consequences.

Despite the risks of friendship and love, Winston and Julia strike up a secret relationship. They tryst for months before settling on a regular spot, a room they rent above a dilapidated antique shop. Together, they pledge allegiance to the Brotherhood, a highly secretive resistance organization, through a mutual acquaintance in the Inner Party. Throughout this time, Winston is waiting to be discovered and tortured, which does come to pass as their contact turns out to be loyal to the Party and the ultimate architect of their undoing.

After months of torture in the Ministry of Love, Winston is released a different, broken man. He is no longer a threat to the Party, having betrayed

Julia to save himself. We leave Winston in a café, watching a telescreen, as he realizes once and for all that "he had won the victory over himself. He loved Big Brother" (p. 284).

Little Brother by Cory Doctorow

In *Little Brother*, high school senior Marcus, alias w1n5t0n, uncovers a Department of Homeland Security (DHS) plot to imprison people in the name of preventing terrorism. A deadly terrorist attack sets off a chain of events in the Bay Area of the United States, which becomes a police state under the rule of the DHS. Marcus and his friends—Darryl, Vanessa, and Jolu—are captured after trying to get help for Darryl, who was stabbed in the melee after the attack. They are brutally interrogated under suspicion of terrorist involvement. After days of mistreatment, Marcus is finally released. He returns home to his worried parents, but realizes quickly that his computer has been bugged and his whereabouts are being closely monitored by the shadowy DHS. More worrisome is the fact that Darryl is still nowhere to be found.

Marcus puts his expert computer skills to work in exposing the DHS and locating and freeing his still-imprisoned friend. He creates a network of trusted young hackers by distributing burned discs that allow those in the circle of trust to connect without fear of interception or surveillance. The network, Xnet, is infiltrated by a DHS spy, and Marcus must turn to other creative solutions for bringing down the corrupt DHS and freeing Darryl.

Marcus attempts to engage the press in a virtual press conference but fails to get his message across. Ultimately, Marcus decides to trust local reporter Barbara Stratford, who starts working on his story. In the meantime, Marcus arranges a game for hundreds of Xnetters called the VampMob, where he plans to unify young hackers and set the DHS up to look bad in the media. The VampMob goes awry, and after escaping once and "going underground," Marcus is captured and taken to the secret prison he calls Gitmo-by-the-Bay. Marcus and the other prisoners are liberated by the California Highway Patrol after Barbara Stratford's story comes out.

BEFORE READING

Defining "Dystopia"

As a genre, dystopian science fiction offers the reader a vision of a futuristic society that feels both familiar and alien. Dystopias take contemporary ideas or concerns and push them into the future as a way to warn about the dangers of particular actions and behaviors. Common themes in dystopias focus on governmental control, lack of personal freedoms, or danger from scientific or technological change. Before reading the novels, provide students with a definition of utopia and explain that dystopias are the opposite of utopias. Ask them to define dystopia based on the definition of utopia. Then ask them to share the names of dystopian novels, television shows, and movies and create a class list. Ask students to look across their list of texts and create a list of four or five characteristics of dystopias. This list should include ideas such as an all-powerful government, society rebuilt in the aftermath of war, use of technology to control or manipulate people, and so on. As they read the two novels, they will likely recognize the characteristics they developed.

Several key themes link *1984*, *Little Brother*, and contemporary culture: surveillance and privacy, technology and power, and propaganda and protest. The activities that we suggest for use before, during, and after reading the novels highlight those themes and ask students to explore ethical issues raised in the texts.

Contextualizing the Novels

Before beginning the texts, introduce the students to the historical and technological contexts of the two works. In particular, students should focus on understanding the genre of dystopian science fiction and the historical context of both novels. Understanding the context of the times will help students understand society's view of technology, people, government, and privacy.

Both *1984* and *Little Brother* are examples of dystopian science fiction in which the reader is offered a vision of a world gone terribly wrong. Hill (2012) defined a dystopia as

> a futuristic society in which a system has been constructed to allay the ills that pervade our present, such as poverty and overpopulation. On the surface this system, through advanced technology and/or other means, appears to benefit the populace, but on closer examination, citizens are worse off. (p. 101)

What present ills are these texts responding to? Contemporary geopolitical events occurring when *1984* and *Little Brother* were published (in 1949 and 2008, respectively) informed the writing of the novels, and knowledge of these events will give the reader insight into key features of the texts. Technology was or could be used to spy, kill, or control information, and it is easy to see how those technologies could be used in destructive ways. As readers, it is important for students to understand the fears of totalitarianism and terrorism that thread through the texts. Both texts respond to the geopolitical climate of the world in which they were written by imagining a scenario in which technology is used to control and track the people. In order for the students to understand the context, have them research the following questions:

- What major geopolitical events happened in the years before the publication of each work? In particular, students should focus on the rise of totalitarianism and mass surveillance, and on the formation of the U.S. Department of Homeland Security after the 9/11 attacks. Wikipedia has helpful pages on these events as a starting point.
- What predictions can students make about how/if these events will have an impact on the content (plot, topic, choice of protagonist/antagonist) of the novel? Students should record their predictions and revisit their answers as they begin reading the texts.
- Who are the authors, and what perspectives might they have and/or leave out? For example, what are their racial, ethnic, class, and other identities? For basic author information, students can look at Wikipedia and other web resources. For further information, Orwell has been the subject of several biographies, and Doctorow has an extensive online presence (blogs, social media, interviews, etc.).

Based on what they learn about the time periods and conflict, students can use that information to speculate on how these events may inform the story's development. As they read the novels, they will be more attuned to themes and events that mirror or address concerns of the time period. After gathering information from the web and/or other history resources, students can then create an infographic that makes a claim about the contexts surrounding the writing of the novels and provides evidence from their research. The infographic should contain the question the students were attempting to answer, the sources they used to create their answers, and information that provides both answers to the question and clear evidence of student thought and engagement, along with compelling visuals (images, symbols, color schemes). To create digital infographics, students can use a variety of free online infographic and graphic design programs like Piktochart and Canva.

The Question of Privacy

Both texts focus on surveillance and the violation of privacy. As a pre-reading activity, ask students to respond to the following questions: *How do governments, corporations, and individuals surveil us and each other? Do we have a right to privacy?* After students have responded, put them into teams to discuss their ideas. Ask each team to report and then, as a whole class, discuss the ideas presented. Ideally, students will present multiple sides to the issues. If they do not, ask them to develop the counterargument to what they have shared. The goal of this activity is to help the students see that issues around surveillance and privacy are already part of their lives.

DURING READING

What's in a Name?

The titles of these texts hold special significance. In the case of *1984*, Orwell was imagining a possible future in the year 1984 as he wrote it. Teachers can ask students to discuss the role that titles play in helping readers make sense of the context and plot of the novel. "Little Brother" is a reference to the "Big Brother" from *1984*. Students can consider why the title uses "little" brother instead of "big." How does this direct reference and connection to *1984* add meaning and insight to the reading of *Little Brother*? The naming connections do not end at the title. Marcus uses the alias w1n5t0n, which is a nod to the main character of *1984*. Students can read Doctorow's bibliography (p. 379) to see how he describes the influence of Orwell's novel on the writing of his own.

Connecting the Texts to Each Other and Today

As we see by reading Doctorow's bibliography and uncovering naming connections between the two novels, these two texts are deeply related to one another. To gain a better understanding of both texts, we explore connections—both similarities and differences—between them. *Little Brother* is explicit in its naming connections to *1984*, but there are other thematic associations as well. As you read, ask students to develop a chart where they find themes and terms that are common to both works and make further links, as applicable, to modern-day examples. Students can use the following table (figure 6.1) as a graphic organizer for making connections among Orwell, Doctorow, and contemporary culture.

Technology, Privacy, and Surveillance

In an essay on technology and creativity, Doctorow (2006) stated, "Technology giveth and technology taketh away" (n.p.). He explained that technology provides new creative options and new kinds of audiences for writers, creators, artists, and performers. Technology makes it possible to bring the arts into people's homes, but it also can violate traditional expectations of privacy or copyright. The same technology that makes it possible for people

Term/Idea/Name	*1984* by George Orwell	*Little Brother* by Cory Doctorow	Contemporary Connections
Big/little Brother	"On each landing, opposite the lift shaft, the poster with the enormous face gazed from the wall. It was one of those pictures which are contrived that the eyes follow you about when you move. BIG BROTHER IS WATCHING YOU, the caption beneath it ran" (p. 3).	Title is reference to big brother, but using little brother implies someone is watching but that things might be different in this incarnation.	*Big Brother* is the title of a popular TV franchise, and "Big Brother is watching you" posters are widely available.
Government control	The Party runs a deeply totalitarian state where they control everything, down to citizens' words and even thoughts. They regularly capture and torture citizens suspected of infidelity to the regime (even for "thoughtcrimes").	The Department of Homeland Security (DHS) illegally detains and tortures citizens in the name of preventing terror.	Examples are US government use of waterboarding, examples of "re-education camps" in North Korea, DHS sending agents in unmarked vans to detain protestors in Portland, OR.

Figure 6.1 **Example of a Graphic Organizer Entry Connecting *1984* and *Little Brother*.** Created by authors.

to communicate and share with others around the world is also the same technology that makes it possible for them to be surveilled by governments and corporations and lose personal privacy. If we consider an example from the present day, we can see the ways technology is used to identify, follow, or avoid particular groups of people. The murder of George Floyd sparked international protests against police brutality and demonstrations in support of Black lives. Protestors and the police alike use technology (video cameras, twitter, Facebook, Instagram, etc.) to identify people or report behaviors. Because bystanders shared cell phone video on social media, the public can see what happened to George Floyd. The actions of the police cannot be hidden because there is now public record shared widely on multiple platforms. Because there are recordings of the protests from city cameras and from protestors who have posted them, police can also use facial recognition software to identify and track participants; this could be used to create a database of protestors. In an eerily similar scene to Marcus and his friend's capture by government agents in unmarked jeeps (p. 39), protestors in Portland, Oregon, have reported being tracked and captured by federal officers in unmarked vehicles, and the DHS has confirmed their involvement in these captures (Levinson et al., 2020).

Both *1984* and *Little Brother* illustrate multiple instances in which the characters lose their personal privacy because they are constantly being watched by the technology that surrounds them. The emphasis on surveillance is so strong in *1984*'s Oceania that children are encouraged to spy on the adults in their lives and turn in family members for transgressions. Likewise, the technology in *Little Brother* is used to follow students, to identify their thinking and possible actions, and to encourage them to betray their peers. However, the two depictions differ importantly in that technology is also seen for its liberatory potential in *Little Brother*.

Surveillance and Privacy

As a pre-reading activity, we asked students to begin thinking about the right to privacy, which is an important thread to follow while reading both texts. In particular, these texts offer rich opportunities for exploring relationships among technology, privacy, and surveillance. In *1984*, Outer Party members like Winston are constantly surveilled. Telescreens allow the government to see and hear everything they do, even at home. Children are trained to spy on and turn in their parents for flouting the rules. There is a sense that everyone is watching your behavior, ready to turn you over to the authorities for the tiniest infraction including "thoughtcrime"—a Newspeak word for impure or anti-party thoughts. Much of the tension in the novel arises from the fear of discovery—of Winston's diary, of Winston's own thoughts, and of Julia's and Winston's meeting places—that hinges on an idea of private space, thought, and action as deviant in the ever-watchful eyes of the Party.

In *Little Brother*, Marcus engages readers directly with his views on privacy, but there is contradiction between his words and actions; he argues for the right to privacy from DHS (or other) surveillance, but he then proceeds to violate others' privacy by stealing their data with his "arphid cloner" (Flanagan, 2014, p. 147). This raises questions about the link between privacy and civil rights. For example, is it okay to violate privacy in service of upholding other rights, and who makes those decisions about what is acceptable? There are governmental agencies who say yes and have what they see as valid reasons for this, but others disagree. Take, for example, debates over whether Apple should be forced to provide access to phones of people suspected of committing crimes, which Apple has so far declined to do.

Complicating the Anti-Technology versus Pro-Technology Narrative

Surveillance technology is an intrusion into daily life and privacy in both novels. In *1984*, Julia, Winston, and other Party members are objects of surveillance, only finding potential escape in remote natural settings far from technology. Although government surveillance technology plays a central role in *Little Brother* as well, Marcus has a much more agentic relationship to technology. He is both the victim of and perpetrator of technologically enacted scrutiny, and Doctorow's narrative is "innovative in its portrayal of computer hacking as a valid type of resistance to this type of [government] surveillance" (Flanagan, 2014, p. 131). Marcus is a hacker, using technology to thwart unwanted surveillance and re-establish his access to private spaces. When tinkering with his ParanoidXbox, Marcus says,

> The best part of all of this is how it made me *feel*: in control. My technology was working for me, serving me, protecting me. It wasn't spying on me. This is why I loved technology: if you used it right, it could give you power and privacy. (p. 88)

This power is not always clearly benevolent, however; his hacking leads to ethical questions and complicates the relationship with technology. For example, if you violate privacy for a "higher good" or to combat oppression, does it make it just? Marcus violates other people's privacy while he uses his "arphid cloner," but he does it for a purpose he deems worthy (Flanagan, 2014, p. 147). Students can debate about whether they believe this is just and justified, even though it violates Marcus's commitment to digital privacy.

Too often, readers position themselves and the texts as either pro-technology or anti-technology. This binary position may lead to critical positions that are hard to maintain. Marcus has a right to privacy, *but* he is also violating someone else's rights. Looking at these two texts side by side can help students complicate good/evil views of technology. They can examine how characters function as active agents or passive objects with regards to technology, and how that might shift across technologies. For example, Marcus identifies as a hacker and has deep knowledge and control of communication technologies. He believes that "Computers can control you or they can lighten your work—if you want to be in charge of your machines, you have to learn to write code" (Doctorow, 2008, p. 120). On the other hand, Winston is largely at the mercy of his technology and those who control it, hiding from telescreens to write in his own home (see p. 7). Students can also examine how the technology shapes the users just as the users shape it. Perhaps Marcus is able to be more of a successful hero because he can create his own software to accomplish his goals, while Winston shrinks away from the technology that controls him; technology drives opportunity for one character, while trapping and punishing the other.

The technology in *Little Brother* is ostensibly used to help teach the students or to keep them safe, but it is also the technology that is used to surveil them. There is a balance here between the liberatory uses of technology and control. As students read *Little Brother*, ask them to identify the technology used in Marcus's life inside and outside of school. How is he surveilled by this technology? Ask students to create a chart of the technology, its intended

Technology Name and Description	What is it designed to do, and how is it used and/or abused in the text?	Connections to Existing Technology
Telescreen in *1984*: a two-way screen that is both a projection device and a surveillance device	The telescreen is designed to connect party members, broadcast propaganda, and spy on people in their homes. It is a key instrument of surveillance, indoctrination, and control in *1984*, and Winston grows to loathe and fear it.	In-home virtual assistants and video-chatting and, more broadly, the "internet of things," where devices and appliances in your home are connected to the internet
SchoolBooks in *Little Brother*: Marcus describes SchoolBooks as the "snitchiest technology of them all, logging every keystroke, watching all the network traffic for suspicious words, counting every click, keeping track of every thought you put out over the net" (Doctorow, 2008, p. 14)	SchoolBooks, originally designed to provide textbooks and tools for students, is also a tool used to monitor their behavior and actions.	Schools and workplaces use tracking and filtering software.

Figure 6.2   Examples of Technology Found in the Texts. Created by authors.

purpose, and its actual use. As they create the chart, ask the students to think about parallel technologies in their current life (see figure 6.2). Some technologies to consider include the arphid cloner (p. 46), facial and gait recognition (p. 18), encryption (p. 152), and networking/DNS (p. 278) in *Little Brother*, and the memory hole (p. 36), the speakwrite (p. 36), microphones, and other Records Department technology for creating telescreen programs and fake images (p. 41) in *1984*.

In contrast, the characters in *1984* must escape technology completely to experience any sense of liberation: Winston and Julia carefully journey to a remote countryside spot to tryst away from spies and cameras. Can we imagine a way that Marcus and Julia could have used technology—rather than running from it—to achieve freedom? Perhaps if Winston could hack a telescreen, he could fool his watchers. Or if he could communicate freely with other resistors through encrypted messaging, things could have been different for him.

Technology and Power

For this activity, students should begin to think beyond whether a technology is good or bad and consider instead the ways in which even the most seemingly benign technology can be used in dangerous ways. Instead of asking if the technology is helpful or hurtful, they can ask how technology might be weaponized for the sake of power. Ask students to choose a technology that they use every day and consider how it supports them. Then have them determine how that technology could be used to control, manipulate, or damage them if it was used by someone trying to gain power. If students need an example of this, they can focus on how a technology such as Instagram can be a way to communicate with others and share moments in your life. However, it can also be used to bully others or to manipulate how we see people, products, or events.

Tracing Technology

Both *1984* and *Little Brother* use technology as a device to further the plot or to establish context. Students could make a list of the technological gadgets and processes in the novels and consider which of them are now realized. After these have been charted, ask students to consider the question, *In what ways are current technologies different from the technologies in the novels? For example, how do our computer and TV screens compare to telescreens in 1984? Are the representations of technology realistic or familiar?* Students can make notes of their answers to these questions in a simple two-column note chart.

Propaganda

Both novels raise questions about what makes a statement or an account the truth or a lie. Students should consider who is given the power to make the decision about which accounts are true and which are false and why it matters to the characters or to the plot. In *1984*, Winston's job at the paradoxically named Ministry of Truth is to rewrite documents so that they align with the Party's version of history. The Party uses the slogan "Who controls the past . . . controls the future: who controls the present controls the past" (Orwell, 1949, p. 33). This idea, when enacted, means that the Party controls how people know of events and how those events do or don't get remembered. In *Little Brother*, Marcus attempts to use the press to control the narrative that is being spread about the actions he and his peers took. Students can consider how/if both of these instances describe the use of propaganda, defined as something that "compel[s] an audience to believe as indisputable conclusions which do not present a complete set of relevant facts and circumstances" (Kim, 2007). In teams, they can build a case for why certain messages in the text (e.g., Marcus's press conference, the Party's broadcasts) should be considered propaganda, addressing what the "indisputable conclusions" and the incomplete set of facts are. Next, they can discuss what this might look like if presented in a way that would *not* be considered propaganda. For example, how might a more neutral journalistic source present the information as disputable and more complete (if it is possible to do so)? Ask students to present their cases and "counter cases" to the whole class.

Language, in particular, is a key propaganda tool in both *Little Brother* and *1984*. As students read, they should revisit their key terms chart and consider the question, *How has 1984 influenced the language, characters, and plot of Little Brother?* They should discuss how linguistic choices reflect the historical moment of the text. Both texts incorporate key ideas and information from the time in which they are written. For example, students could explore the meaning and presence of "terrorism" in *Little Brother* and newspaper articles from the end of World War II, the 9/11 terrorist attack in 2001, and today. Present debates surrounding when to label a violent act "terrorism" or its perpetrator a "terrorist" have exposed deep racial and religious prejudice in America. For example, there is debate over whether and when white supremacist violence in the United States is considered "terrorism" (e.g., see Allen, 2020).

To understand more deeply how propaganda is constructed, ask students to create their own propaganda video or poster for the Party, using visuals and Newspeak. Alternatively, students can create a public service announcement from Marcus's or another hacker's perspective, revealing how the DHS uses propaganda to skew public opinion and hide their misdeeds.

AFTER READING

Both *Little Brother* and *1984* focus on dystopian futures and provide insight into the very real possibilities of technology as a tool of control, surveillance, and propaganda. Considering how the protagonists in the canon novel and the contemporary young adult novel fail or triumph in their efforts to resist unjust regimes allows readers to analyze the characters' actions and imagine their own possible ones. As students critique the novels' portrayals of protest and rebellion, can they make connections to current events? How does technology serve as a tool of both enslavement and freedom?

Protest and Rebellion

In both novels, the protagonists fight against overly powerful government forces. They rebel against these forces in ways large and small. Winston protests by writing in his diary and by meeting with Julia. He refuses to give over his mind to the Party until he can no longer resist. Marcus organizes the VampMob and wages a hacking war against the DHS. Both face grave danger for these actions. After reading both novels, students have two models of what protest and rebellion might look like in the face of totalitarian control. Students could use a Venn diagram in order to compare and contrast the justifications and methods of exerting control that the Party and the DHS use. Students should then consider if they believe the methods of control have any connection to the protagonists' different approaches to resistance. In small teams, ask students to discuss the following:

- What responsibility do individuals and/or groups have to object to a system they believe is unjust?
- How do these protagonists rebel? What are the results and costs of their rebellion, and should that calculate into their decisions to fight or follow?

They should consider the questions and use evidence from the texts to answer: *How and where do they see Marcus and Winston justify their action or inaction with their own moral reasoning? How do they involve others in efforts to create collective action, and how do they work alone?* Students should examine sections in *Little Brother* or *1984* if they get stuck.

One major difference to highlight is the role of technology in the protagonists' rebellion. While Winston seeks to escape the telescreen, Marcus embraces his hacker identity to use technology to his advantage; in this way, Winston seeks freedom *from* technology and Marcus seeks freedom *through* it. This further underscores Doctorow's complication of the anti-technology narrative that is so often present in young adult novels, dystopian novels, and in the media. Rather, technology can be a conduit for power and social activism for both the "big brothers" and the "little brothers" of the world.

Current Events Connections

The novel *1984*'s ideas and language have become a large part of our language. Although teachers and students will have noted several examples of the prevalence of "Big Brother" around us, students will be able to find new examples from current media sources as well. The government and news media, for example, may have competing narratives about the COVID-19 pandemic. Students can bring in relevant news articles, Twitter feeds, and other media tools to show the competing narratives. Additionally, they could find a recent example of an Orwellian word in modern use in a journalistic source.

The Year

Students can also consider questions around what happens when the year named in the title of the book occurs: *How visible was the book 1984 in the year 1984?* For example, the students can view and analyze Apple's 1984 Super Bowl advertisement (Bloomberg, 2014). In the advertisement, a woman launches a sledgehammer into a screen filled with Big Brother's face, blowing the screen up as drone-like, gray-clad men watch. The ad ends with the text "On January 24th, Apple Computer will introduce Macintosh. And you'll see why 1984 won't be like '1984.'" In a subsequent interview, Lee Clow, who worked on the famous ad, discusses how they intentionally subverted the idea of technology resting in the hands of the powerful, offering the revolutionary Macintosh as technology for the people. Apple is now a top global technology company, and its products have massive global reach. Students could examine how the advertisement uses the themes of surveillance and social control to make a point about technology. *How do the themes potentially help sell the branding of the company? What does the message at the end, quoted above, mean and why was it so powerful for audiences?*

Becoming Critical Readers

These texts mirror many of the challenges of contemporary society. As readers, we see patterns of behavior in these texts that connect to or reflect contemporary questions. Within the past ten years, there has been increased attention on how people of color are treated by people in authority and in schools. This attention has allowed teachers and readers to talk about normalized behaviors within a society and within a society reflected in texts. Considering what behaviors are normalized in *1984* and *Little Brother* challenges readers to think critically about the texts. Students should ask the following questions:

- What is considered "normal" in these texts, and how do you know?
- How are the characters and their actions shaped by their race, class, gender, or religion?
- What would constitute a non-normative identity in *1984* or in *Little Brother*?
- Are there representations of non-normative identities?
- How do the texts succeed in challenging ideologies in some ways, but fail in others?

Look, for example, at the discussion of the roles of slaves, proles, and other minorities in maintaining the structure of the Party and Oceanic society in *The Theory and Practice of Oligarchical Collectivism*—a fictional book within *1984* (p. 198). In *Little Brother*, Marcus talks about his white privilege:

I didn't ask to be white. I didn't think I was being braver just because I'm white. But I knew what Jolu was saying. If the cops stopped someone in the Mission and asked to see some ID, chances were that person wasn't white. Whatever risk I ran, Jolu ran more. Whatever penalty I'd pay, Jolu would pay more. (p. 160)

Marcus is clear that he did not have to consider his own race in choosing his path for resistance but he is aware that Jolu would have to do so. *How does race affect the decision to resist in certain ways in the novel?* Both novels raised questions about the treatment of characters based on their race. Winston and Marcus are white males and with that comes some privilege in their respective societies. In thinking about their privilege, consider how other characters were controlled or marginalized by what was considered normal for the society in the text.

Technology creates both new possibilities and new inequities in these texts. As readers, examine how technology creates new possibilities for the characters, paying special attention to those characters who are traditionally marginalized. Students can also link their ideas about characters in the texts to modern protest movements with large online components, like Black Lives Matter and #MeToo. As these examples show, technology has become a tool to support social protest. For a deeper exploration of "networked protest," search for Zeynep Tufekci's work (including articles, interviews, videos, and her book *Twitter and Tear Gas*).

EXTENSION ACTIVITIES

Power to the Youth

In *Little Brother*, Marcus starts a youth social movement that ultimately helps bring down the powerful and corrupt DHS. One of his slogans is "Don't trust any bastard over 25!" (p. 166). Youth both marginalizes and empowers Marcus and his friends in the novel, but ultimately they prevail over the DHS by force of will, collective action, and shrewd alliances with select adults (like Barbara). Ask students to think about why Doctorow might have chosen to make Marcus a teen hacker and to list the tactics that make Marcus and his friends successful (like hacking skills, connections to trusted adults, ability to organize using technology, for starters). *How do the youth-organizing tactics relate to current youth movements?* For example, young people have been crucial in fighting against climate change or in arranging protests in support of social movements. How are those movements similar to or different from the actions of Marcus's hackers?

Intellectual Freedom

The quest for freedom of thought and speech are important threads running through both novels. Students can use Marcus's and Winston's ideas about these freedoms to start an investigation into what "intellectual freedom" means today. *What is intellectual freedom, and how is it protected—or not— in your country and across the world?* Students can start with resources at the American Library Association's intellectual freedom advocacy page, or explore on their own. Discuss how social media, new technologies, and widespread surveillance have changed how we talk about intellectual freedom.

More Extension Ideas

To extend engagement with the ideas and language of these texts, students can explore surveillance technology, research internet privacy and freedom, analyze social media, and create multimodal projects. Some possible activities are as follows:

- Conduct a "surveillance audit" and create an interactive map of places where students see surveillance technology. Students should think about who is surveilling them, why, and how.
- Read the privacy policy and the rules/community norms of a favorite social media app/site in small groups. How is private information shared/protected? Who owns it? What kinds of speech are allowed, and what kinds are not?
- Explore the Electronic Frontier Foundation and create a series of ads or posters explaining their mission.
- Follow an author such as Cory Doctorow whose professional policy runs counter to traditional expectations of copyright. Doctorow, as part of his artistic stance, makes his creative works available digitally at no cost. Consider how Doctorow or an author like him creates a digital presence across multiple media platforms.

CONCLUSION

Like all good dystopian science fiction does, *1984* and *Little Brother* offer us glimpses into scary and dangerous potential futures. The techno-totalitarian futures imagined in these texts seem more haunting than many of the imagined futures in science fiction because the themes are realized in much of our daily lives. More than 50 years separate these novels, and yet the political climates that generated these texts seem remarkably palpable and realistic in their familiarity. *Little Brother* provides both a counterpoint and a connection to the prescient message about action in the face of immorality delivered in Orwell's *1984*. Orwell, in response to critique of his novel, stated, "The moral to be drawn from this dangerous nightmare situation is a simple one: Don't let it happen. It depends on you" (Packer, 2019, n.p.). As readers, we have the option to use these terrifying visions to imagine a future that looks different from the dark ones that Orwell and Doctorow describe.

REFERENCES

Allen, J. R. (2020, February 24). White supremacist violence is terrorism. *The Atlantic*. Retrieved from https://www.theatlantic.com/ideas/archive/2020/02/white-supremacist-violence-terrorism/606964/.

Bloomberg. (2014, December 3). *The real story behind Apple's famous '1984' Super Bowl ad* [Video]. YouTube. https://www.youtube.com/watch?v=Psj MmAqmblQ.

Doctorow, C. (2006). Science fiction is the only literature people care enough about to steal on the internet. *Locus Magazine*. Retrieved April 4, 2020, from https://craphound.com/content/Cory_Doctorow_-_Content.xhtml#section_12.

Doctorow, C. (2008). *Little brother*. New York, NY: Tor Books.

Flanagan, V. (2014). *Technology and identity in young adult fiction: The posthuman subject*. New York, NY: Palgrave Macmillan.

Hill, C. (2012). Dystopian novels: What imagined futures tell young readers about the present and future. In J. Hayn & J. Kaplan (Eds.), *Teaching young adult literature today* (pp. 99–115). New York, NY: Rowman & Littlefield.

Kim, S. S. (2007). Propaganda. In *University of Chicago Theories of Media Keywords Glossary*. Retrieved from https://csmt.uchicago.edu/glossary2004/propaganda.htm.

Levinson, J., Wilson, C., Doubek, J., & Nuyen, S. (2020, July 17). Federal officers use unmarked vehicles to grab people in Portland, DHS confirms. *National Public Radio*. Retrieved from https://www.npr.org/2020/07/17/892277592/federal-officers-use-unmarked-vehicles-to-grab-protesters-in-portland.

Make Orwell fiction again tote. (n.d.). In *American Library Association Store*. Retrieved April 3, 2020, from https://www.alastore.ala.org/content/make-orwell-fiction-again-tote.

Orwell, G. (1949). *1984*. New York, NY: Harcourt Brace and Company.

Packer, G. (2019, July). Doublethink is stronger than Orwell imagined. *The Atlantic*. Retrieved from https://www.theatlantic.com/magazine/archive/2019/07/1984-george-orwell/590638/.

Transhumanism and post-reality. (n.d.). Retrieved from https://cot.gbcnv.edu/~schwandt/S10_FPs_pub/John_S/transhuman.html.

Chapter 7

Identifying and Interrogating Toxic Masculinity in *Lord of the Flies* and *The Chocolate War*

Katharine Covino, Anna Consalvo,
and Natalie Chase

Toxic masculinity refers to "the constellation of socially regressive male traits that serve to foster domination, the devaluation of women, homophobia, and wanton violence" (Kupers, 2005, p. 714). While it does not mean that "all men are evil, and they are to blame for all the negative things that exist in this world" (Hall, 2018, para. 3), toxic masculinity is one aspect of Western culture that warrants critical scrutiny. And what better way to exercise this scrutiny than through the safe distancing of literature.

Ashlee et al. (2018) claimed that toxic masculinity "describes the harmful impacts of masculinities that emphasize dominance, the use of violence to solve problems, and the suppression of empathetic emotions, like sadness, fear, and compassion" (p. 73). Central to a paradigm of toxic masculinity, according to Berdahl et al. (2018), are values that include aggressive competition and complete control of those deemed weaker (p. 423). In this worldview, "real men" are those who rise in positions of power through the subjugation of others (p. 426). Markers of masculine performance, according to Yarrow (2018), include what men *do*—lead, provide, protect—and also what men *don't*. Contending that "real men don't cry, don't talk about their feelings, don't give up, don't avoid a fight if provoked, aren't 'sissies,' aren't passive, [and] aren't vulnerable," Yarrow drives the point home that "real men" are not caregivers or nurturers—the very notion is anathema (2018, p. 62).

Populated mainly by male characters and settings that highlight male-centric isolation, competition, and violence, the conflicts that arise in *Lord of the Flies*, by William Golding (1954), and the young adult novel *The Chocolate War*, by Robert Cormier (1974), are results of cultures of hyper-masculinity, or, in 2020 terms, "toxic masculinity." A prominent shared theme among these novels is the deep (and deeply troubling) association between power, domination, and the characters' enactments of toxic masculinity. Through this text pairing, in this chapter we offer students the opportunity to think about both durable and malleable cultural imperatives around conceptions of masculinity from a perspective of gender theory (O'Donovan, 2006). Our central goal is to create a safe and richly textual environment where students can deeply and critically consider culturally inscribed, gendered performances of femininity and of masculinity. As so many classic texts are centered on "Western, white, heterosexual masculinities" and as "it is important to consider how masculinities interact with nationality, culture, sexuality, gender identity, class, and other aspects of difference" (Ashlee et al., 2018, p. 73), an essential outcome we hope to foster is to help students become aware of falsely monolithic, essentialist viewpoints, thus enabling them to use their own voices, thoughts, experiences, and ideas to drive their own analyses and discoveries.

Lord of the Flies by William Golding

In *Lord of the Flies*, British prep school boys, young adolescents (approximately 10–13 years old), are marooned on a tropical island after a plane crash in which the adults are killed. The leadership gap is filled by Ralph—a preteen who attempts to care for and lead the boys, and who struggles against increasingly strong waves of brutality. Written shortly after World War II, Golding's setting draws from experiences and conceptions of masculinity from the era. Featuring central characters who initially strive to embody an amalgamation of traditionally masculine and feminine traits and practices, Ralph soon emerges as the central character. Though only 12 years old, he stands out among the small group of isolated children for his maturity, leadership, and forward-thinking abilities. As the de facto leader, he is initially able to practice and embody both conventionally masculine and feminine traits. For example, seeing a conch shell on the beach, he decides to use it to find other boys and call a meeting. During this first meeting, he becomes chief of the boys through a peaceful, democratic vote and allots jobs and responsibilities to his newly formed tribe. Later, as they explore the island, he claims all the land. These examples (and many others) illustrate ways that, initially, Ralph enacts an identity as a leader that entwines the traditionally feminine traits of caregiving, nurturing, and empathy together with the traditionally masculine traits of strength, independence, and decisiveness. The grim circumstances of the second half of the novel, however, demand a significantly altered gendered performance—one that requires Ralph to rid himself of any hint of vulnerability, compassion, or empathy.

The Chocolate War by Robert Cormier

Cormier's novel reflects the postwar quest for a suburb-striving population. *The Chocolate War* takes place in a Catholic high school for boys in a working-class, industrial city in the northeast. Simmering under the surface of jobs, homes, and private school lurks hunger for power and control of others through intimidation, physical domination, and subterfuge. The school's headmaster is taken ill and his place is filled by the power-seeking Brother Leon. Both the presence and influence of adults, however, remain only in the shadowy background. Real control of the boys' lives lies in the hands of The Vigils, a school gang. Under the leadership of ruthless Archie Costello, and using any means available, they work both independently and with Brother Leon to dominate teachers and students.

The reader experiences Cormier's world through the novel's protagonist, 14-year-old Jerry Renault. Jerry is a dreamer who cherishes his friends, grieves for his mother, and longs for a life of self-actualization guided by his own decisions and choices. As the novel moves forward, Jerry becomes increasingly aware of the darkness in his school, which emanates from both The Vigils and the complicit adults who enable them. In the final fight with Vigil enforcer Emile Janza, Jerry is forced to abandon his last shreds of caring—for himself, or for anyone else. He is consumed by "the sickness of knowing what he had become, another animal, another beast, another violent person in a violent world" (Cormier, 1974, p. 254). In that terrible moment, Jerry becomes a living embodiment of toxic masculinity.

BEFORE READING

To read and understand *Lord of the Flies* and *The Chocolate War* through a lens of toxic masculinity, students must first understand and be able to apply a number of larger theoretical concepts, gender key among them. Teachers interested in supporting their students in this scholarly work should lead them through the following before-reading activities. The first activity looks at gender theory broadly and positions gender theory as an overarching umbrella that sits above and encompasses all performances of masculinity—including toxic masculinity. Engaging in this first activity, teachers can use the quick review of feminist and post-structuralist theories outlined below to help students understand, define, and apply gender in new ways. This first activity will also help students begin to understand the interplay between gender and power. Then, having helped students create for themselves a revised conceptualization of gender, teachers can lead them into the second before-reading activity. Much like the preliminary exploration of gender, the second before-reading activity incorporates theory, but quickly moves toward a more concrete, hands-on application. Guided by the central thrust of two texts, this second activity zeroes in quickly on various performances of masculinity—including toxic masculinity. Where the first before-reading activity is inward-facing and asks students to engage in introspective reflection, the second before-reading activity is outward-facing and asks students to review a short text through the critically aware lens of gender theory. Both before-reading activities will prime students for successful reading and analysis of the two central texts and will enable students to transfer their awareness of gender-related issues to other texts and the world around them.

Understanding Gender Theory

Given the age, maturity, and life experiences of many secondary students, it may be difficult to dive right into the topic of toxic masculinity. Teachers interested in easing their students toward these potentially challenging themes more gradually can take a step back and begin their examination of gender from a more accessible place. Before reading either of the central texts, *The Chocolate War* and *Lord of the Flies*, teachers can engage students in a discussion of gender more broadly by offering a short mini-lesson on gender theory, presented here. Though there are many different ways of understanding "gender," in the context of this chapter we conceive of gender as (a) fluid and dynamic, changing amidst different settings, contexts, people, attitudes, and beliefs; (b) a social creation, at times a social performance and at other times a social practice; and (c) a social construct.

Teachers interested in helping students to understand gender in this feminist, post-structuralist way can encourage them to consider their own gender identities. For example, to help students appreciate the ways that gender is "flexible, fluid, and sometimes contradictory" (Blaise, 2005, p. 99), teachers can ask students questions about the divergent ways they practice gender in their own lives. Some adolescents may struggle with this new way of understanding gender. Some may even protest, arguing that gender is always fixed. Offering the image of a teenage girl as a graceful ballerina, a nurturing babysitter, and an aggressive soccer player can help convey how gender can be "fluid, negotiated and constructed across different social and cultural contexts" (Jackson & Gee, 2005, p. 116). These types of conversations should help students to understand that gender is not fixed, static, or predetermined, but rather "forever shifting and evolving" (Myhill & Jones, 2006, p. 100).

Just as gender is dynamic and fluid, it is also contextually determined. That is to say, ideas about gender, such as gender roles and gender performances, can and often do evolve based on changes in context or setting. Gender performances also change depending on the "who" present—who is "in the audience," so to speak. In this sense, gender is relational. What gender looks like—the right way of "doing" gender—exists as an open system of relationships and contexts in constant motion. Perhaps Orellana (1999) summed it up best offering "an understanding of gender as constructed, shaped through relations and practices, and enacted through multiple, contradictory positions assumed in different contexts within specific relations of power" (pp. 111–12).

To help students understand the links between gender, context, and power, teachers can again ask students to think of a time when they felt they were "doing gender" right or when they felt they were "doing gender" wrong. Teachers can further hone the conversation by asking students to consider a time when they felt empowered (or disempowered) by their gender. While there are innumerable examples that might spur the conversation forward, one or two possible anecdotes might help students get on the right track. Teachers could ask students to consider times when their gender made them feel "like a fish out of water." For example, in contemporary American culture, a high school boy trying to join an elective class on cosmotology or a high school girl trying out for the football team might feel as though they stand out. Of course, there is nothing wrong with either of these scenarios. The boy or girl in these examples may feel out of place, or at the very least be aware that they are pushing societal gender norms. These short prompts, and others students generate and share, will help to spur a rich and complex discussion where students will be able to apply their growing knowledge of gender theory and explore the links between gender and power, preparing students to take up the gendered themes presented in both novels.

Exploring Toxic Masculinity

Because masculinity stands at the thematic heart of the two novels, *The Chocolate War* and *Lord of the Flies*, teachers can gradually shift the conversation from a broad discussion of gender toward a focused look at masculinity. As with gender, it makes sense for us to share briefly our conceptual understanding of toxic masculinity. Ashlee et al. (2018) offered a helpful and succinct conceptual definition of toxic masculinity as one that "describes the harmful impacts of masculinities that emphasize dominance, the use of violence to solve problems, and the suppression of empathetic emotions, like sadness, fear, and compassion" (p. 73). Yarrow (2018) added to this definition, contending that social norms dictate that "real men don't cry, don't talk about their feelings, don't give up, don't avoid a fight if provoked, aren't 'sissies,' aren't passive" (p. 62). In other words, men—real men, that is—are never vulnerable and never afraid. To bolster this point, the author cited a 2016 YouGov poll wherein 75 percent of men revealed they felt "social pressure to 'act strong' even if they feel scared or nervous inside" (Yarrow, 2018, p. 65). Taken together, these sources make clear that toxic masculinity is a performance of masculinity built upon hyper-masculine traits, including dominance, violence, subjugation, and suppression. In this practice of masculinity, there is no room for nurturing, empathy, compromise, or care for others.

"We Believe: The Best Men Can Be"
Engaging with Toxic Masculinity

To help focus the conversation on masculinity, instructors can share the short Gillette (2019) advertisement "We Believe: The Best Men Can Be" with students. After viewing, teachers could distribute index cards and ask students to generate three products: one question, one comment, and one real-world connection. Teachers may find that students have strong reactions to this short video. To ensure freedom of expression while at the same time facilitating collegial discussion, teachers are encouraged to set some simple ground rules for class discussion. In creating and sharing these guidelines with students, teachers may encourage use of "I statements" for expressing personal reactions. Further, they can encourage suggestions rather than imperatives to fellow students.

The Gillette advertisement offers a window into differing performances of masculinity and how American society's expectations of masculinity have changed over time. As such, it is likely to evoke a broad range of responses from students. Some students may be open to considering the message of the advertisement. They may ask questions like, Why do adults use the excuse "boys will be boys" to justify poor or bad behavior? Contrastingly, other students may feel defensive. They may see their own gendered lives reflected in the short commercial—and not in a positive way. For example, when the authors shared this activity with students, one young man asked, "'Boys will be boys' is how most were raised. Was it a bad way to raise a boy? . . . This is how me and my cousins were raised." No matter how students react to the advertisement, it is important to honor and include their voices and perspectives. There is not a right answer here. Rather, the discussion should serve to (a) build upon the students' growing knowledge of gender theory and (b) help students understand that different performances of masculinity reflect different sociocultural norms and power dynamics.

The goal of this activity is for students to walk away from this portion of the activity with the understanding that gender and power are linked, but that those links are not set in stone. Teachers can close this activity by directing students to the online comments associated with the video, where a quick review reveals that the number of negative comments is more than double the number of positive comments. Instructors can ask students about this disparity. Guiding students through the process of synthesizing their own views and the views of others can help them understand and appreciate diverging perspectives of gender—not only those that relate to this video but also, more broadly, including those at work in their own lives. While student responses to the negative comments about the advertisement will differ, we will offer one exemplar from our own teaching here that touches on some key points. Early in her response, a female student mused that "people are afraid. They're afraid of expression, they're afraid of other's opinions, they're afraid of being wrong, they're afraid of unwinding the way things have been for so long and they're afraid of being targeted." Many of the fears that she identified are dominant forces in how society and its members determine who is "acceptable" and who is "the other"—not just "the other," but often "the lesser" (O'Donovan, 2006). Gender performances or views on gender that fall outside society's bounds have the potential to expose those who hold or exercise them to reprisal and punishment. Williams (2006) put it more bluntly: those who do not agree with the prevailing views on gender "will be shut out and shunned" (p. 301). Helping students unpack and understand the Gillette advertisement and probe questions of gender and power supports their understanding of various performances of masculinity at work in *The Chocolate War* and *Lord of the Flies*.

DURING READING

To guide students through a deep and thoughtful exploration of the differing shades of masculinity at work in the paired texts, including toxic masculinity, teachers can begin by focusing on *Lord of the Flies*. By looking at this text first, teachers can help students understand masculinity through the lens of various literary devices used throughout the novel. Through the multiple steps suggested below, teachers can guide students through scaffolded activities, ensuring that they build upon their prior knowledge as they progress through the novel. Identifying character traits and imagery (Chapters 1–4) before moving on to more the complex tasks of examining symbolism, allusion, and allegory (see figure 7.1) will serve to support students' reading comprehension and analysis of textual performances of masculinity. Each new step builds on the literary analysis of the one before it, and each presents students with a task that gradually increases in challenge. By the end of their reading for *Lord of the Flies*, students should be familiar with characterization, imagery, symbolism, allusion, and allegory, as each literary device demonstrates and reflects varying performances of masculinity. Though this set of activities is designed for *Lord of the Flies*, teachers should find that they can also be applied to a

Examples of Imagery in Chapters 1-4
"He came at last to a place where more sunshine fell".... all the way to the end of the page through "Their scent spilled out into the air and took possession of the island" (Chapter 3, p. 47).
"Roger stooped, picked up a stone, aimed, and threw it at Henry—threw it to miss" and continue to "Roger's arm was conditioned by a civilization that knew nothing of him and was in ruins" (Chapter 4, pp. 51-52).
"He peered at his reflection and disliked it"…through…"Bill started up laughing; then suddenly he fell silent and blundered away through the bushes" (Chapter 4, p. 53).
Examples of Symbolism and Allusions in Chapters 5-8
"Things are breaking up"… through… "Then people started getting frightened" (Chapter 5, p. 70).
"You, Simon?"…through…"Inspiration came to him" (Chapter 5, p. 77).
"Ralph was dreaming"…through… "…feeding the ponies with sugar over the garden wall" (Chapter 6, p. 86).
"This head is for the beast"…through…."…through the forest toward the open beach." (Chapter 8, p. 122).
"There isn't anyone to help you"…through…."Why things are the way they are?" (Chapter 8, p. 128).
Examples of Allegory in Chapters 9-12
"Kill the beast!....through.... "…the tearing of teeth and claws" (Chapter 9, p. 136)
"At last Ralph stopped"…through… "You ought to know that, Ralph" (Chapter 10, p. 139).
"His voice rose under the black smoke"…through to… "…wise friend called Piggy" (Chapter 12, p. 182).

Figure 7.1 Imagery, Symbolism, Allusion, and Allegory in *Lord Of the Flies.* Created by authors.

subsequent reading and analysis of *The Chocolate War*. By guiding students through these steps, teachers can prioritize deeper analysis and gradually add layers of complexity for students to consider as they read first *Lord of the Flies* and then *The Chocolate War* through the lens of masculinity.

Understanding Masculinity through Character Analysis

Differing performances of masculinity are present in both *Lord of the Flies* and *The Chocolate War*. The total focus on male characters, however, does not mean that characters are all alike; far from it. Further, it does not mean that the male characters are static and unchanging. Many of the characters develop and change throughout the course of the texts. For some characters, the change is clear. For others, the change is more subtle. But nearly all character evolution trends in the direction of toxic masculinity, either embodying it or noting its growing power within the group. More specifically, there seems to be a pattern in both texts that reveals characters, most particularly protagonists, struggling in their performances of gender. Though the protagonists initially seek to embody and practice both masculine and feminine traits, ultimately, they are forced to shed themselves of any nurturing, caring, or emphatic instincts in order to maintain a leadership role, or even to survive.

Example: Selecting One Character

To begin exploring the links between character portrayal and masculinity, teachers can advise students to each select one character from *Lord of the Flies*. Students will follow this character throughout the novel and engage in close textual analysis to trace changes in the ways that character performs gender. Specifically, students will be responsible for analyzing their own character deeply and keeping a record of significant quotations, moments of important dialogue, character traits, and symbols that relate to that character and his gender performance. Of course, this does not mean that students cannot analyze other characters besides the one they are assigned: they are simply responsible only for keeping a record of one character. At the end of each chapter, the students will share with the whole class or with a small group what they have identified and discovered about their characters. The teacher can use the students' findings to compile an evolving chart of all the characters' traits, important quotes, and performances of masculinity that can be used for notes, as a model, or to revisit later on. This during-reading activity aims to encourage students to analyze the characters deeply and to critically engage with their gendered performances.

For example, students could explore the character of Simon. Many students are usually able to analyze Jack or Piggy's character, but students may need more guidance with more complex characters like Simon. The recommended passage that illuminates Simon's character is taken from Chapter 3, "Huts on the Beach," and begins with "He came at last to a place where more sunshine fell" and continues for four paragraphs until "Their scent spilled out into the air and took possession of the island" (p. 47). Analyzing Golding's techniques and style in this passage reveals a great deal about Simon's character. He is quiet and sensitive. He prefers solitude and peace. Though he sees and loves the natural world, he keeps his connection to nature a secret. He knows that his awareness of the beauty and the stillness of the island separates him from the other boys. His underlying sensitivity and goodness causes the group to first overlook and then ostracize him. Simon's interconnectedness with the island and his self-reflective character allow him, and the reader, precognition of the growing horror and brutality. This example makes clear the possible insights students can gain by critically examining characters through the lens of masculinity.

Using Imagery to Explore Masculinity

Exploring and unpacking imagery is a critical component of all textual discussion. While many rich and complex images exist in *Lord of the Flies* and *The Chocolate War*, none are more pertinent to the work of this chapter than those images that demonstrate, convey, and reflect various aspects of masculinity. Indeed, one thing that is striking about both novels is how the authors use rich, abundant imagery to reveal and expose underlying truths of their characters. The way they describe a character's appearance, for example, can help students understand that character's practice of masculinity and how that practice of masculinity fits into the world created by the larger community. Probing the overlaps between character, imagery, and masculinity, this activity builds on the previous one to help students not only recognize intersections between character, imagery, and gender but also explain their significance.

This during-reading activity focuses on the early part of *Lord of the Flies*, specifically Chapters 1–4. As the students move through these chapters, they will be asked to highlight or make note of significant imagery-laden passages that display something about the characters and their differing personality traits. This activity builds upon the ongoing character analysis work outlined and explained in the previous section. As students move into their exploration of imagery, they will build on each other's findings to help deepen their growing understanding of various characters' gender performances. As they read, students should be able to draw from significant passages in order to display their comprehension of the text and of their growing understanding of the various shades of masculinity at work in the band of boys. After the students complete each section, the teacher can collect and share key images and quotes that add to students' growing understanding of the thread of masculinity that runs through the text.

Example: Using Imagery to Explore Masculinity

As with any activity, it is important that teachers model the process of textual engagement and analysis for students. Providing such an example can help students understand the teacher's expectations and can also offer students insight into the level of engagement that is required. Again, we have chosen to focus on imagery that contrasts Simon and Jack. The recommended passage is from Chapter 4, "Painted Faces and Long Hair," and begins at "He peered at his reflection and disliked it" and continues for a page and it concludes with "Bill started up laughing; then suddenly he fell silent and blundered away through the bushes" (p. 53). The title of this chapter foreshadows the slow but inexorable descent toward savagery among the pack of boys. They begin by masking their true identities. When Jack smears the clay on his face and creates this mask, he makes this transformation clear. Stepping away from humanity and civilization, he is moving toward a new way of being, one that Simon and some of the others are unable to relate to. Focusing on imagery, students can see in their mind's eye Jack's new face, now clay-white and red and black. This depiction of Jack suggests the mounting change in his character; he has not fully succumbed to the savagery of which he is capable, but he is halfway there. Comparing and contrasting Golding's uses of imagery in descriptions of Simon and Jack conjure different moods. The Jack passage evokes darkness, whereas Simon's passage above feels illuminated. As the novel progresses, Jack sinks deeper into savagery. Encouraging students to analyze character through image, as modeled above, will help them move past mere summary, and to engage critically and evaluatively with the text. Such analysis of character through imagery will prepare students to analyze character through the lens of masculinity.

Unpacking Masculinity through Symbolism, Allusion, and Allegory

Both *Lord of the Flies* and *The Chocolate War* offer rich and varied examples of figurative language. Of particular note are the powerful and complex instances of symbolism and allusion, both of which present readers with potent allegorical connections. In the past, these stylistic choices have been linked to larger themes in the text and subsequently read (and taught) through historical lenses and biblical lenses. Here, we offer a different lens—that of masculinity. By looking closely at various examples of symbolism, allusion, and allegory in the latter half of *Lord of the Flies*, students can continue to build upon knowledge they have gained in their explorations of character and imagery. Indeed, it is not possible to understand more complicated instances of figurative language without first gaining an appreciation of more accessible elements of story. Synthesizing what they have learned, students can begin to understand how literary devices convey and reflect the author's views on the world—and the way men can (and should) exist in it.

By this point in the unit, students should be able to read passages and critically engage with character and imagery, particularly as each relates to masculinity. The goal is for teachers to lead students toward unpacking these more challenging devices—symbolism, allusion, and allegory—by using the knowledge that they have acquired in the previous activities. Each section of this unit scaffolds towards the next. With each new activity, teachers are setting students up for continued success by slowly adding depth and rigor. Now that students have read about half of *Lord of the Flies* and are able to complete close readings of significant passages, they will be able to move on to the latter half of the novel, focusing on more complex literary techniques and a deeper level of analysis. Teachers can begin guiding students in the process of evaluating the symbolism and allusions embedded in the text for purpose and depth. The allusions and symbolic moments that are present in these chapters can help the students classify the main characters and continue to analyze them using the skills they have learned in these lessons. At this point in the unit, students should be ready to engage with symbolism and

allusion in conjunction with imagery to help identify the differing practices
of masculinity among the characters.

Example: Symbolism, Allusion, Allegory, and Masculinity

Because these literary concepts may be more challenging for students, it is
critical that teachers provide examples from the text and then, with students,
practice deconstructing those examples together. This collaborative engagement will not only help students refresh their understanding of the definitions
of these literary terms but also guide them as they apply them to the text
through the lens of masculinity. Here we recommend a collection of three
passages from *Lord of the Flies*. Each of these sections presents a different
conceptualization of Simon's death and what it means to the community of
boys. Overlaying and synthesizing these passages, teachers can help students
see not only the omnipresence of toxic masculinity but also what it costs
characters to embody and inhabit it.

The first passage is taken from Chapter 9, "A View to a Death," and begins
with "*Kill the beast! Cut his throat! Spill his blood!*" and continues down the
page until "There were no words, and no movements but the tearing of teeth
and claws" (p. 136). The second part of this trilogy is taken from Chapter
10, "The Shell and the Glasses," and begins with "At last Ralph stopped. He
was shivering" and continues in a dialogue-rich exchange down to "Not all
that well. I only got one eye now" (pp. 139–40). Completing this threesome
is a short, descriptive paragraph from Chapter 12, "Cry of the Hunters," that
begins with "His voice rose under the black smoke . . ." and continues to ". . .
the true, wise friend called Piggy" (p. 182).

Taken together, these passages outline the devolution of the boys'
morality. They are blinded by their own fear and are unable to distinguish
make-believe from reality, action from consequence, and humanity from
monstrosity. In killing Simon, the boys finally give in to the bloodthirsty
playacting that mirrors their shared dark desire. Seen in this light, the murder
and its aftermath represent a moment of climax and a point-of-no-return. By
killing Simon, the boys kill their own purity. They destroy their last links to
childhood, goodness, and redemption. When he breaks down weeping, Ralph
is clearly mourning the loss of his friend, but on a deeper level, he is mourning the loss of his own innocence and boyhood in which care, nurturing, and
empathy were possible. What the boys have killed in their brutal ecstasy is
the chance to inhabit any form of masculinity other than toxic masculinity.
Drawing from such passages, students can build an argument for characters
and the actions they pursue as not only symbolic but allegorical micro-myths
that tell a dark story of the loss of humanity.

Synthesizing Differing Practices of Masculinity in *Lord of the Flies* and *The Chocolate War*

The consideration of toxic masculinities shown in each text has been, up to this point, separate. In this fourth during-reading activity, students bring in what they know about gender and about both novels' characters. After students have read and analyzed each of the texts and have a well-developed understanding of the ways in which character, imagery, symbolism, allusion, and allegory work to reflect varying performances of masculinity, they are invited to synthesize their views of characters in both novels, together. Using a spectrum, teachers can ask students to locate where characters fall in relation to each other. By locating on a continuum the key characters from both novels, students examine masculinities through comparison and contrast, providing textual evidence for each choice. The line of the continuum begins at the far left in the most toxic zone, called "exploitative," moves in a rightward direction to the moderate "accommodating" sector, on to a "sensitive" region, and, finally, to "transformative" territory (Herrera & Prosnitz, 2016, p. 11). This structure offers students four broad categorizations with which to analyze characters' behaviors. Students will decide which characters belong in any given category, provide textual evidence for their selections, and add annotations to the continuum. Teachers can offer students the opportunity to add subcategories or even to rename the major categories.

Example: Continuum Map of Masculinities

As with other teaching examples, it is important for teachers to model this process for students. They can do so by tracing the character of Jack. For example, in *Lord of the Flies*, it is Jack who first strays from the mission of the group by ignoring his duty toward the continued nurturance of the signal fire (pp. 36–37, 44, 59) who becomes obsessed with hunting (pp. 44–45, 60), and through whom violence is first seen when he hits and essentially half-blinds Piggy (p. 60). One way of describing Jack's role in the novel is that of key villain, which falls within the "exploitative" zone (see figure 7.1). After locating the key villain character of Archie in *The Chocolate War*, students could then consider ways in which Archie is similar to and different than Jack. Archie's specialty is psychological terror as opposed to Jack's overwhelmingly physical intimidation. Archie smoothly and frighteningly feigns friendliness in his cat-and-mouse interview with Goober (pp. 28–29). Archie controls the Vigils enforcer, Janza, whom he finds repugnant and whom he calls "beautiful," by keeping an incriminating photograph of Janza and using it like a carrot-and-stick (pp. 42–43) device. The students' mastery of these characters and their psychological traits will provide them insight as they place the characters on a spectrum, weighing their practices of masculinity against those of other characters in both *Lord of the Flies* and *The Chocolate War.*

AFTER READING

Guiding readers through each of the activities, teachers have helped their students find new ways of applying gender theory and masculinity to their reading of the texts. Through their engagement with the texts, students have gained practice identifying and exploring passages in which character traits, imagery, symbolism, allusion, and allegory work with and through each other to convey the authors' ideas about who men are and who men should be in the world. Now, the work of the after-reading activity is to build upon students' abilities to apply what they have learned through a creative assessment that calls upon both critical analysis and synthesis of the performance of masculinities throughout the paired texts. This culminating after-reading activity asks students to consider the entirety of a single character's gendered portrayal, and then to create a mask that represents the various ways that character embodies and practices masculinity throughout the novel.

The Fractured Self: Probing Performances of "Mask" Ulinity

Throughout many pieces of literature, it is common for characters to put on a facade in order to fit in, adapt, and even survive. Such facades, or masks, allow characters to choose how the world sees them. In both *The Chocolate War* and *Lord of the Flies*, many of the characters wear masks, although different characters use masks in different ways. Each boy, through a process of curating his own identity, forges a delicate balance of forefronting and sublimating differing aspects of his inner self. The work of creating and wearing their masks empowers these boys to exist within peer groups that value toxic masculinity.

In this after-reading activity, ask students to choose a particular character from either *The Chocolate War* or *Lord of the Flies*. With their chosen character in mind, students can dig more deeply into that character's identity performance. To do this, students can review the notes, quotes, and other materials they have gathered, and begin to deconstruct the character's performances of masculinity throughout the text. The product for this after-reading activity will consist of two parts: a mask and an accompanying piece of writing. First, students creatively construct a mask that portrays various aspects of the chosen character's identity and performance of masculinity. Accompanying the mask is a well-developed short analysis that further showcases the students' understanding of the components of the mask using the language of gender theory and masculinity. Using at least one specific literary element from this unit, students focus on imagery, allusion, symbolism, or allegory in both their mask and analysis.

Example: Probing Performances of "Mask" Ulinity

Teachers should model the process of mask making and analysis for students. For example, teachers can highlight the ways that Jerry, from *The Chocolate War*, gradually changes over the course of the novel. Here, we recommend a set of paired passages that highlight the different performances of masculinity Jerry embodies, first at the start, then, at the close of the novel.

The first passage is taken from Chapter 3, and begins with "Hey, man" and continues through a rather long exchange across two pages to "He looked up at the advertising placards above the windows, wanting to turn his thoughts away from the confrontation" (pp. 19–20).

The twin to this first passage is from Chapter 37 and begins with "The kid wouldn't go down" and then continues through the half-page to "He had allowed Archie to do this to him" (p. 183).

Taken together, these passages trace Jerry's trajectory from a thoughtful and considerate youth to vengeful and violent animal. The paired sections also reveal Jerry's keen awareness of the change within himself. The descent toward toxic masculinity, though necessary for his survival, costs him his very personhood. In the first passage, Jerry's exchange with the drifter shows his initial compassion and connection to others. At the beginning of the novel, Jerry is sensitive, caring, and aware of the possibility for reflection and growth in himself and others. The first passage reveals him to be a person who, by his own admission, hates conflict and confrontation. At this early point in the novel, it seems as though Jerry is aware of a great narrative, but unsure how to access it. Full of potential, he is poised at the edge of metamorphosis. Later in the novel, as shown in the second passage, Jerry is crushed by the machine of violence operated by The Vigils and Brother Leon. He learns that the only way to survive is by masking his inclinations toward self-reflection, connection, and empathy. Like Golding's Ralph, Cormier's Jerry is self-aware and sees growing evil within himself, yet tragically unable to return to his own prior innocence. Guiding students toward the latter part of the novel and its dark closing chapters, teachers can demonstrate why Jerry must stifle and subsume his gentler side beneath a brutal, toxic masculinity.

EXTENSION ACTIVITY

Extending means to go farther, to go longer, to go deeper, to open up. The main goal of this extension activity is to build upon students' growing understanding of gender theory and masculinity by asking them to look beyond the text and to apply what they have learned to the real world.

Exploring the Spectrum of Masculinities through Images

In preparation for the activity, the teacher can create a bulletin board with the spectrum of masculinities, reflecting the information in figure 7.2. Teachers can ask students to bring in a picture of a boy or a man that they do not know. Beyond this prescription that the image be anonymous, students should be given freedom to find whatever image they would like. Images can come from magazines, newspaper articles, or online sources. With this picture in hand, students can perform a basic critical discourse analysis to identify various markers or indicators regarding the pictured person's performance of masculinity.

Then, using the information in figure 7.2, students could then present their analysis to the class. Accompanying each student's presentation of their selected individual, teachers can lead the class in a discussion where students decide where on the spectrum of masculinity the pictured person lies. The class should make this decision together and then pin their images on the bulletin board. As each student shares their picture and critical discourse analysis, the class can discuss where the person in the image belongs on the spectrum and why. The point of this exercise is not to have one correct answer. Instead, the purpose is to engage in real, multisided discussion in which students prove their growing progress, growth, and mastery of gender theory and the spectrum of masculinity through thoughtful, dynamic discussion. While this bulletin board can live in the teacher's own classroom, it is

Novel	Villainous	Enforcer	Protagonists	Companions	Pacifists
LOTF	Jack	Roger	Ralph	Piggy	Simon
TCW	Archie	Janza	Jerry	Obie	Goober
Exploitative → Accommodating → Sensitive → Transformative					

Figure 7.2 Spectrum of Masculinity in *Lord of the Flies* and *The Chocolate War*. Created by authors.

also possible to create a more outward-facing display. A bulletin board in a main hallway could serve as the source for a school-wide discussion or event, with the students who engaged with the unit on gender-theory and masculinity serving as knowledgeable ambassadors for their peers.

CONCLUSION

Of course, space is a limiting factor in what this chapter can offer. This rather small unit could be expanded or taken up in phases. One suggestion is to select more texts written in 20-year intervals - that is, similarly themed literature from around 1994, 2004, and 2014 to follow the thread of cultural replication and cultural change as it plays out across decades. For such an exploration, adopting a lens of new historicism (Robson & Greenblatt, 2007) could be helpful to establish consistent vocabulary in the examination of social behaviors and mores across time. Additionally, to further the breadth and depth of these conversations we suggest that teachers thoughtfully bring in, as exhibits for students' guided consideration, texts from current popular debates around toxic masculinity, including those from social media, blogs, news stories, and published articles. Additionally, using lenses such as psychoanalytic literary criticism with a focus on Freud's (1923) concepts of id, ego, and superego to study character development and motivation could help a classroom community grapple with the continuum of masculinity, from vulnerable/positive to bulletproof/negative.

REFERENCES

Ashlee, K., Spencer, L., Loeffelman, M., Cash, B., & Muschert, G. (2018). Fostering critical awareness of masculinity around the world. In G. Muschert, K. Budd, M. Christian, B. Klocke, J. Shefner, & R. Perrucci (Eds.), *Global agenda for social justice: Volume one* (pp. 73–80). Bristol University Press.

Berdahl, J. L., Cooper, M., Glick, P., Livingston, R. W., & Williams, J. C. (2018). Work as a masculinity contest. *Journal of Social Issues, 74*(3), 422–48.

Blaise, M. (2005). A feminist poststructuralist study of children "doing" gender in an urban kindergarten classroom. *Early Childhood Research Quarterly, 20*, 85–108.

Cormier, R. (1974). *The chocolate war.* New York, NY: Bantam Doubleday.

Freud, S. (1923/1964). The ego and the id. In James Strachey (Ed.), *The standard edition of the complete psychological works of Sigmund Freud, volume XIX (1923–1925): The ego and the id and other works* (pp. 1–66). Hogarth Press.

Gillette. (2019). We believe: The best men can be | Gillette (Short Film). In *YouTube*, https://www.youtube.com/watch?v=koPmuEyP3a0.

Golding, W. (1954/1999). *Lord of the flies.* New York, NY: Penguin-Putnam.

Hall, C. (2018, February 1). Why toxic masculinity does not mean what you think it means. *Elephant Journal* [online]. https://www.elephantjournal.com/2018/02/why -toxic-masculinity-doesnt-mean-what-you-think-it-means/.

Jackson, S., & Gee, S. (2005). "Look Janet," "no you look John": Constructions of gender in early school reader illustrations across 50 years. *Gender & Education, 17*(2), 115–28.

Kupers, T. A. (2005). Toxic masculinity as a barrier to mental health treatment in prison. *Journal of Clinical Psychology, 61*, 713–24.

Myhill, D., & Jones, S. (2006). "She doesn't shout at no girls": Pupils perceptions of gender equity in the classroom. *Cambridge Journal of Education, 36*(1), 99–113.

O'Donovan, D. (2006). Moving away from "failing boys" and "passive girls": Gender meta-narratives in gender equity policies for Australian schools and why micro-narratives provide a better policy model. *Discourse: Studies in the Cultural Politics of Education, 27*(4), 475–94.

Orellana, M. F. (1999). Language, play, and identity formation: Framing data analyses. In B. Kamler (Ed.), *Constructing gender and difference* (pp. 97–117). New York, NY: Hampton Press.

Robson, M., & Greenblatt, S. (2007). *Routledge critical thinkers.* New York, NY: Routledge.

Williams, B. T. (2006). Girl power in a digital world: Considering the complexity of gender, literacy, and technology. *Journal of Adolescent & Adult Literacy, 50*(4), 300–7.

Yarrow, A. (2018). Masculinity, mating, and misogyny. In *Man out: Men on the sidelines of American life* (pp. 61–84). Washington, DC: Brookings Institution Press.

Chapter 8

Fallen Angels and *The Things They Carried*

Bringing the Vietnam War to Light

Crag Hill

War is a constant, today and throughout written history. Carried by story long before the invention of writing, war has now been a frequent subject in young adult (YA) literature for decades. Name a war and there is probably an award-winning YA novel exploring the impact of it on young men and women and their family, friends, and community. The Revolutionary War: Christopher Collier and James Lincoln Collier's (1974) *My Brother Sam Is Dead* and Laurie Halse Anderson's (2016) "The Seeds of America" trilogy. The Civil War: Irene Hunt's (1964) *Across Five Aprils*. World War II: Joseph Bruchac's (2005) *Code Talker*, Markus Zuzak's (2005) *The Book Thief*, and Sharon Cameron's (2020) *The Light in Hidden Places*, among so many others. Vietnam War: Walter Dean Myers' (1988) *Fallen Angels* and Thanhhà Lại's (2015) *Listen, Slowly*. Iraq War: Patricia McCormick's (2009) *Purple Heart* and Walter Dean Myers' (2008) *Sunrise over Fallujah*.

These YA novels humanize these wars, putting faces on the dates, people, and places mentioned, sometimes only in brief, in history textbooks. Rather than simply telling us what happened, they immerse us in the experiences of the men and women who suffered and survived the challenges of combat, who fought and died, and those who returned to a life they often found unbearable to live. For the authors of *Fallen Angels* and *The Things They Carried*, Walter Dean Myers and Tim O' Brien respectively, these novels helped them to resolve some of the emotional issues they were struggling with long after their service. For adolescent readers today, these novels provide a window to look at historical conflicts while helping them construct a lens to view the conflicts that arise during their lifetimes. What they learn through reading these novels can inform decisions they may need to make or positions they may need to take in the future.

I have taught *The Things They Carried* to both sophomores and juniors; it always topped the list of favorite novels on the survey we administered to graduating seniors to assess our literature program. Many of my students would then pick *Fallen Angels* from my bookshelves when they wanted to know more about Vietnam. I have taught *Fallen Angels* in numerous young adult literature courses (among other Walter Dean Myers novels) over the last 20 years. These two novels have resonated in both teaching contexts because it seemed in every class students had an uncle or aunt, a grandfather or grandmother, or some other relative who served during the Vietnam War or, more recently, in Iraq and/or Afghanistan, and many of my students, young men and women, were prepared to join the military following graduation themselves. These two novels offered these readers insight into the experiences of their loved ones, experiences that many veterans continue to be reluctant to talk about if at all.

The Things They Carried by Tim O'Brien

The Things They Carried is a genre-bending work of fiction. Is it a novel or a collection of short stories set in the United States and in Vietnam before, during, and after the war? Is it creative nonfiction or memoir, the main character sharing the name of the author? The book gives you an inside view of the Vietnam War from the points of view of a character named Tim O'Brien and other men who served, all with complicated and confounding reasons for serving, as well as the story of one singular woman, MaryAnne, who embraces the experiences of war like no other character. The episodic narrative depicts O'Brien's ambivalent engagement with the conflict beginning with being drafted after completing college, through his discharge because of wounds received in battle, to his life as a veteran and father following the war. Other characters play prominent roles, though some make but brief appearances. Some characters readers will not forget are Kiowa, O'Brien's closest friend, who died a gruesome death; Norman Bowker, whom readers will spend a Fourth of July with following the war as he circles a lake in his hometown, unable to move his life forward; the platoon's medic Rat Kiley, the colorful storyteller who recounts (or concocts) the story about Mark Fossie's high school girlfriend, Mary Anne Bell, who according to legend disappears into—or becomes—the jungle.

Fallen Angels by Walter Dean Myers

Fallen Angels' 17-year-old Richie Perry has a lot in common with Tim. Though he enlisted in the army, he too is ambivalent, drifting into the war as he passively awaits a medical discharge because of a knee injury he sustained in a basketball game at home. Richie had ambitions to go to college and become a writer like James Baldwin, but he felt he could not afford it and did not have anything else to do, not wanting to get caught up in the gangs on the streets of Harlem. Richie's squad is sent on numerous dangerous missions, each one more brutal than the previous mission, bringing out the best and worst in the men. As with *The Things They Carried*, many of the characters are memorable for their courage both in battle and with their feelings toward war, as well as for their wacky sense of humor, which helped many soldiers cope. His friend Peewee will especially stand out for his wit and bluster. To cope with his experiences in the war, movie-enthusiast Lobel amuses Ritchie by "writing" what is happening or could happen to the platoon in a movie script. Though neither Mama or Kenny, Ritchie's younger brother, are developed as characters, their importance to him will endear them to the reader.

NOTABLE FOR TEACHERS

I would suggest that teachers not introduce one novel as an adult novel and the other as a YA novel. If that distinction is made by students, so be it. But naming novels in this way often impels readers to judge one as better than the other (adult novels are more complex, more sophisticated, we hear again and again) before they even have read it. I argue that these novels are equals; they both immerse us in the lives of men and women and move us emotionally and intellectually, neither inherently more nor less. Either novel could be read first in a unit. The second novel would be enriched by the previous reading and understanding of the first novel would be expanded during the reading of the second novel. Neither is easier or harder.

BEFORE READING

Setting Up the History

Despite the fact that the fall of Saigon (now Ho Chi Min City) and the Vietnam War took place decades ago, very few people were untouched. As such, it is important to take the time to set the context. Along with print resources there are hours and hours of audio and visual material on the history of these wars available online. The most comprehensive, of course, is Ken Burns and Lynn Novick's 10-episode, 18-hour documentary "The Vietnam War." In lieu of viewing that entire epic, teachers could have students explore the material available on History.com. To help students build ownership of the material, a jigsaw reading of may be effective. Count students off by 6. Assign all 1's the first two short texts and the embedded videos, "Roots of the Vietnam War" and "When Did the Vietnam War Start". Number 2's will read the next two texts, number 3's the next two, and so on until all 12 topics have been covered. Before teams form that include students, one from each number, have the students first meet in expert groups, that is, all students who read the first two texts meeting to share what stood out for them in the material they read and viewed, clarify any confusion they may have, and together deciding what are the main points to share with their classmates. The combined teams, consisting of a mixture of students numbered 1–6, can create a timeline for the war, as well as log any questions that they have about the war.

Virtual Visit to the Vietnam Veterans Memorial

The Vietnam Veterans Memorial on the National Mall in Washington, DC, recognizes and honors the men and women who served during the Vietnam War. Since it opened in November 1982, The Wall has been visited by millions of people from the United States and around the world. The Wall, as of May 2019, is comprised of inscriptions of the names of 58,276 service members who died or are still missing in action. The Vietnam Veterans Memorial Fund has designed a virtual tour of The Wall, which includes the history of the design and stories about the items left at The Wall. Because of the emotional impact The Wall engenders, taking the virtual tour following the work on the war's historical background as a whole class is suggested. This will offer a collective as well as an individual experience of the Vietnam War and its legacy.

The Things Students Carry

The first chapter of *The Things They Carried* is "The Things They Carried." The soldiers all carried a variety of necessities (can openers, mosquito repellent, cigarettes, salt tablets, wristwatches), but then they also carried items that were particular to them, letters, a diary, the New Testament, tranquilizers, and Dr. Scholl's foot powder. Along with their weapons, they all carried steel-centered, nylon-covered flak jackets, green plastic ponchos, and a pair of jungle boots. They carried their emotions, even those they were afraid to show like their fear of dying. *Fallen Angels* also lists the equipment soldiers carried into combat and describes the emotions they brought with them to Vietnam as well as those that arose from their experiences.

This pre-reading exercise will begin to connect students to the soldiers in the two novels, both materially and emotionally. Ask students to list the things they carry to school on their persons and/or in their backpacks. Ask them to write about why they carry these items. *What personal meaning do they have for them? How are they important to their mission at school?* Ask them also, as much as they are willing, to list the emotions they carry into school. *How are these emotions different than those they carry outside of school?* The list might include phones and other electronic devices, headphones or earbuds, car keys, makeup, debit cards, as well as more personal items such as stuffed animals, rainbow pins, or clip-on unicorns. The range of emotions, though perhaps not as wide as those soldiers carried, will nonetheless be striking: fear of failure, joy of comradery, and compliance or active dislike of school procedures and policies. Then ask students what they would carry if they had to serve in the military or in an exchange program far from home. *What items would they take with them? Why? What memories of their home will they carry with them? Why?* Have students create a series of Instagram posts that feature photographs of these items and/or images they create to depict the memories.

Letter Writing and Reading

For all wars since writing was invented, letters have been a lifeline between those serving during war and their family and friends at home. Readers of these letters learn about events, major and minor, but they also learn about how the letter writers felt about them, their fears and hopes; the conditions the letter writers were experiencing, shortfalls of clothing, equipment, and food; and, collectively, what the letter writers wanted their readers to know about—and what they did not (Richie, in *Fallen Angels*, did not speak of the casualties he was witnessing in his letters to his mother and younger brother).

Before viewing excerpts of the 1988 documentary "Dear America: Letters Home from Vietnam," ask students to brainstorm in pairs the kinds of things they would want to communicate to their friends and family if they were serving in a war overseas—and what they would not want them to know. Students may want their family and friends to know that they are safe, that they like and look up to the men and women they are serving with, and that the food sucks. They might not write about the ever-present fear, even in their dreams, and they will not write about any violence they have witnessed.

Select three-to-five-minute excerpts from the documentary that include letters written by those who served. While viewing, have students note the topics the letter writers shared and the topics they didn't. (Revisit this later when Richie writes about what he should or should not write to his mother.) For example, students could view the opening clip. After a montage of video footage from the field, soldiers are shown writing and reading letters. One soldier writes to his sweetheart that he tries not to skip a day in writing her and that whether or not he receives a letter from her depends on if it is a good day or not for him, showing the importance of letter writing in the day-to-day life of soldiers.

Depending on the excerpts, students might be surprised to find that many of the letters recounted funny stories and many were remarkably upbeat. Have students then discuss in groups what the letter writers were feeling about the war and their experiences. What did they get to know about these people? What have they learned about the war from listening to these letters? The answers to these questions will help inform the letters students will be writing below.

DURING READING

Comparing the Quality of Characterization

Both Richie and Tim were members of platoons, a group of 3–4 squads each comprised of 4–20 soldiers, led by lieutenants. In both novels, the lieutenants were prominent characters. There are two lieutenants in *Fallen Angels*, Lieutenant Carroll, who is killed in action and replaced by Lieutenant Gearhart. In *The Things They Carried*, Lieutenant Cross survives the war and meets up with Tim afterward. Richie trusts and respects Lieutenant Carroll, but less so the inexperienced Lieutenant Gearhart. Tim also respects Lieutenant Cross and gets to know him personally, including a window into his love life. Ask students as they read to take note of the physical and emotional characteristics of these men, of the decisions they make or don't make. *What are their leadership traits?* (For example, both lieutenants get to know their soldiers and show a genuine interest in them.) *How do they express their authority?* (Both lieutenants are calm if when engaged in intense combat and give clear direction) *How do they get along and interact with the soldiers?* (Lieutenant Cross is more forthcoming than Lieutenant Cross, even sharing worries about his girlfriend back in the states.) *What do they care the most about?* (Both are determined not to lose a man in an engagement with the Vietnamese.) Create venn diagrams that show what makes the characters different and what traits they share.

As students note the characteristics of each Lieutenant, have them pay particular attention to the quality of the characterization. Ask the class the following to guide them:

- What makes a strong character in a novel?
- What do you need to know about a character's physical description to see them vividly?
- What do you need to know about their actions?
- What do you need to know about what other characters think of them?
- What do you need to know about their emotional life to get to know them intimately?

- Comparing the lieutenants in each of these novels, which character is most complex, more nuanced?
- What are the traits that really stand out?
- Which lieutenant would you want to serve under and why?

After exploring the questions posed above, have students debate which novel has the strongest characterization and what makes that so. For this debate to be rich it is important throughout the unit that the teacher does not mark one novel as adult fiction and the other as young adult fiction, thus, for some readers, implying one is better than another. If that is an important distinction for students let them arrive at that conclusion. Teachers might find that in each class some students will prefer the straight-forward characterization of *Fallen Angels* while others will like the more poetic characterization in *The Things They Carried*. Some students might argue that one is not better, but that each novel takes a different approach.

"Letter" Writing in the Present

During the Vietnam War, people could write letters and postcards, send care packages and telegrams, and make phone calls, though long-distance calls were sometimes cost prohibitive and problematic, and oh, of course, word of mouth. Communication was slow, good news and/or bad news, almost always a little late.

Now there are more ways to communicate with one's friends and family than ever, and communication can be instantaneous, even more so than the telephone in the 1960s, where one usually had to wait for the receiver to get to the phone. We now have text messaging, social media, and videoconferencing, and do not write as many letters or postcards. We can still send the same kind of care packages to our friends and family, but we can now pay to get just about whatever we want to get within hours.

How we choose to communicate reveals something about us, not only the messages we convey but the media we choose to use. For this during reading exercise, a way to deepen connections between the readers and the characters, ask students to select at least two of eight options utilizing communication media from both eras from a choice board:

- Send 10 text messages between characters.
- Film a three-to-five-minute face time session between characters.
- Design and write three postcards.
- Post pictures on Instagram from a character's point of view.
- Send a letter that is written over a —two-three-day time span (not untypical of letter writing at the time—letters could take days to write and cover two to three pages).

- Record a phone call between two characters.
- List the contents of a care package you would send to one of the characters while they were in Vietnam.
- Create messages or video one would post on Twitter, Facebook, or other platforms.

For each of these options, it is important that though the medium is new, the message should still be authentic to the character; for example, both Richie and Tim are introspective and would not reveal too much about themselves in a series of texts (and they both would have followed the conventions of punctuation and capitalization). Have students first share out the messages they have created in groups of four, then share out one to the whole class, discussing how the messages fit the character and what we now understand about the characters.

AFTER READING

As are all war novels that depict combat, both of these novels are exceptionally cinematic. To give students the opportunity to conceptualize a film based on a scene in one of the novels, have students in pairs create an eight-panel storyboard. The first panel should include the title of the scene. For *The Things They Carried* this could be the title of one of the chapters. For example, many students might be intrigued by the story of Mary Anne in the chapter entitled "Sweetheart of the Song Tra Bong." Rat Kiley tells the story of how medic Mark Fossie invited his high school sweetheart Mary Anne Bell to visit him at his medical camp outside the village of Tra Bong and the events that occurred. Students might choose to draw a storyboard that first depicts Mary Anne arriving at the base in pink culottes and sweater, then panels with Mark and Mary Anne spending time together, and Mary Anne learning to care for the patients. But then their story gets darker as Mary Anne begins to go on missions with the Green Berets who use the camp as a base; she is sometimes gone for several nights, much to Mark's distress. The final panel could depict Mary Anne in her pink sweater wearing the necklace of tongues Rat Kiley first saw in the Green Beret's hut.

Among many vivid scenes in *Fallen Angels*, students may decide to create a storyboard for the scene in which Lieutenant Carroll is killed. The panel after the title panel sets the scene, the platoon setting up for an ambush along a path leading to a village that had been harassed by the Viet Cong. In this panel the platoon is cutting brush and filling sandbags, digging in for the long wait. The third panel could depict nightfall, bugs beginning to swarm and frogs croaking. Because it was pitch black, the fourth panel could carry the sounds of the

Viet Cong as they moved down the path toward the village. They were calm, talking in singsong rhythms. The fifth panel could again depict the sounds of the scene, but this now includes an eruption of gunfire. Lieutenant Carroll is hit in the chaos. The sixth panel can show two of Richie's platoon mates carrying Carroll to safety. Carroll is unconscious. The seventh panel depicts the helicopter that takes Carroll and his platoon back to their base. The final panel could show the soldiers kneeling in prayer when they hear that Carroll has died.

This exercise asks students to not only look back into the text but also make decisions on what and how to base a storyboard from which a short film could be made. The exercise also shows the teacher which scenes stood out for the students. It is acceptable if more than one pair focuses on the same scene. The details will vary and can be the springboard for a discussion on how we can view the same scene but describe it in different ways.

Different Plotlines, Different Impacts?

Fallen Angels unfolds chronologically. *The Things They Carried* moves episodically. As an after reading exercise, ask students to construct a plotline for *Fallen Angels,* beginning with decision to enlist and ending with leaving Vietnam. Students should include 15–20 major plot events (e.g., Richie arriving in Vietnam, his first combat experience, the first death he witnessed). Then ask students to map major events from *The Things They Carried* onto the *Fallen Angels* timeline in chronological order as best they can (e.g., Tim O'Brien's decision to go to Vietnam, his first combat experience, the first death he witnessed). As students will see, Richie and Tim share similar events, but the narrative structure—chronologic versus episodic—may create different experiences for readers.

Ask students to write about the effects of each of the narratives. *What effect in The Things They Carried does moving around in time have on the reception of the stories? Why did Myers and O'Brien make these narrative choices? How did the perceived audience of the novels play into their choices, i.e. what kinds of readers prefer chronological plot lines over episodic?* Students have pointed out that because the narrator in *The Things They Carried* is writing from the point of view of an older man that the story has less urgency than *Fallen Angels*, told, as it were, in the moment, but that *The Things They Carried* has more wisdom. Tim O'Brien, students have said, has been reflecting on his wartime experiences for years, while Richie has little time or space for reflection as he is dropped into the middle of intense, incomprehensible experiences from the beginning to the end of the novel. The spaces the narrators are writing from are qualitatively different, yet together they may map onto the experiences of the men and women who served in the Vietnam War more than anyone novel can.

Letters to Characters: An Assessment

Richie Perry and Tim O'Brien would be around 70 years old at this time, each we can imagine having written at least one book about their experiences in the Vietnam War. Imagine that both have been speakers on programs about the war and at one of these events they meet for the first time and decide to meet for breakfast the next day before they leave for home. They have both, of course, read each other's work and have publicly praised it. Over eggs, sausage, and coffee, they click. They retell the stories they tell in their novels, but in the excitement of the telling, they remember more details than they included in the published work. As the pain of the war has grown more distant, their retelling includes the lighter moments they experienced. When they part they promise to stay in touch.

For a possible assessment of student understanding about the characters, ask students to write at least two letters between the two men (one initial letter, say from Richie to Tim, and one responding letter from Tim to Richie). In these letters retell two or three stories from the novels but create the lighter moments that take place before or after the events. One example in writing about Mary Ann Bell, whom Tim could not find any evidence that she existed, Tim might comment that if there were more pink culottes and sweaters in the war it might have gone another way. Richie in response could tell a story about Judy Duncan, the nurse whom he met on the flight to Vietnam. Richie knows that she was killed in action but he wants to remember her as a warm human being, so tells Tim the story she told him about wanting to be a garbageman because the garbage trucks she saw passing on her street were the best things she had seen in her life.

Fact-Finding Mission

Students might have many questions during and after reading these novels. To connect back with the first activity, "Setting Up the History," ask students to write questions they still want to have answered. Here are 20 questions my students have generated as examples:

1. How many people went to Canada and how long did they have to stay there?
2. How many platoons were in the field at any one time in the Vietnam War?
3. What were some of the booby traps made by the Vietcong?
4. How are the Vietnamese and Americans getting along after the war? How are they getting along now?
5. What other countries were involved? For what reasons?

6. Were all the soldiers against the war or were they mostly for it?
7. How many people died or got wounded each year from remaining land-mines in Vietnam?
8. How many people ended up in mental institutions after or during the war?
9. What would people do to stop from going? What were the consequences of dodging the draft? For burning your draft card?
10. How many soldiers returned to the United States and committed suicide?
11. How much were soldiers paid?
12. How many soldiers expanded their service after one year?
13. What was the total cost for the United States for the war?
14. What did average Vietnamese people think about the war?
15. What is Agent Orange? What are its effects on humans?
16. How many are still MIA (missing in action)?
17. How was the weather normally?
18. How long did the war last after the United States pulled out?
19. How many children died in the Vietnam War?
20. How many women were involved? What did they do?

Have them pick 10 of the 20 questions and answer them in as much detail as they can. Post these answers on the class website as FAQs, adding to them each year students read the novel.

EXTENSION ACTIVITIES

Visits from Vietnam Vets

To help students put a face on the war, to bring the past into the present, contact the Vietnam Veterans of America (VVA) organization. As part of their educational outreach, the organization provides lesson plans, handouts, and access to guest speakers who are willing to share their personal experiences virtually and/or in-person. Teachers may be able to make connections with veterans in their community, but VVA is a resource for those communities who may not have veterans available to visit with students. Many of the questions in "Fact-Finding Mission" above will be answered by these kinds of visits.

Researching Local Newspapers

To deepen the understanding of how the war was viewed at home, ask students to access their local newspapers (or archives of newspapers if their community no longer has a newspaper) and research their coverage of the war from 1964 to 1975. How did these papers carry national stories? What local stories did they cover? Did they cover the stories of the men and women from the community who served in the war? If there was a "Letters to the Editor" section in the paper, what were letter writers saying about the war? If students have access to the span of newspapers from 1964 to 1975, did the topics in the "Letters to the Editor" section change over time? As a class, put together a newspaper compiling their findings.

Soundtracks

Wars have always inspired songwriters who composed patriotic songs like George M. Cohan's "Over There," popular during World War I, or protest songs such as Crosby, Stills, Nash, and Young's song "Four Dead in Ohio," recorded just weeks after four students were killed by the National Guard at Kent State in 1970. The Vietnam War inspired more than its share of songs. Students will have heard a sampling of songs in viewing "Dear America: Letters Home from Vietnam," but there are many, many more. PBS, as part of its supplementary resources for the Ken Burns and Lynn Novick's "The Vietnam War," has a page that includes 30-second clips of more than 120 songs included in the film.

Have students count off by nine (there are nine playlists for the 10 episodes located on this webpage; episodes 1 & 2 are combined), and then explore the clips on the playlist corresponding to their number. The first playlist begins with Bob Dylan's "A Hard Rain's A-Gonna Fall." Ask students to listen to the tone of the song as well as the lyrics for this song and for all the others. If the classroom has access to Spotify, they may choose to listen to a song or songs in their entirety, or this exercise could be completed as homework. Have students discuss the following questions in teams: *What is this song communicating about the war? How would Tim, Richie, and their fellow soldiers respond to these songs? For closure have them draft a list of five songs from the documentary that could accompany a reading of each of the novels.*

Knowing that music is a huge part of adolescent lives, ask students to find contemporary songs that invoke the events and experiences of the men and women in the novels. Have them individually prepare a list of five songs and then in pairs have them listen to their partner's songs and try to discern what they represent (before their partners reveal why they chose the song). Have them post these lists on the class website along with the list of songs from the documentary. Alternatively, students could search for contemporary songs that speak to American wars in Afghanistan and Iraq or other traumatic events.

Exploring a Visual Depiction of War

Another extension is to view the many films set during the Vietnam War, including "The Deer Hunter," "Apocalypse Now," "Platoon," "Born of the Fourth of July," "Good Morning Vietnam," "The Killing Fields," and "Birdy." Because these films may require parent permission, this is an extension that may only work at home and with families not averse to graphic depictions of war. Ask students to write a review of one of these films from the point of view of Richie or Tim or from the point of view of both. The writers would address where the films were authentic to their experiences and where they were not.

CONCLUSION

The purpose of teaching about war is first to have students view the conflicts from a safe but critical distant, critiquing the decisions individuals and governments have made in the past. With those critiques as a foundation, students can then question the leaders they encounter in their future lives and the conflicts these leaders may bring the country into. To know about the Vietnam War, the past and present and future cost of this war on human beings and landscapes, will give students multiple lenses through which to see their world.

REFERENCES

Burns, K., & Novick, L. (2017). "The Vietnam War." http://www.pbs.org/kenburns/the-vietnam-war/music/.

Couturié, B., & Dewhurst, R. (2005). *Dear America: Letters home from Vietnam.* New York: Home Box Office video.

History.com. "Vietnam War." https://www.history.com/topics/vietnam-war/vietnam-war-history.

Myers, W. D. (1988). *Fallen angels.* New York, NY: Scholastic Press.

O'Brien, T. (2017). *The things they carried.* Waterville, ME: Thorndike Press.

Vietnam Veterans of America. https://vva.org/.

Index of YA and Canonical Texts

Subject Index

About the Editors

Paula Greathouse is associate professor of secondary English education at Tennessee Tech University. She has coedited several books, including *Adolescent Literature as a Complement to the Content Areas* book series and *Queer Adolescent Literature as a Complement to the English Language Arts Curriculum.* Her research on adolescent literacy and young adult literature have been published in books and top-tier journals such as *Educational Action Research, Study and Scrutiny: Research on Young Adult Literature, The Clearing House,* and *English Journal.* She was a secondary English language arts and reading educator for 16 years. She has received several teaching awards, including the National Council of Teachers of English (NCTE) Teacher of Excellence. She is an active member of the National Council of Teachers of English, International Literacy Association (ILA) and Association of Middle Level Education (AMLE), and is a state representative for the Assembly of Literature for Adolescents of NCTE (ALAN).

Victor Malo-Juvera is a former middle school teacher and is currently associate professor of English education at the University of North Carolina Wilmington, where he teaches young adult literature and multicultural young adult literature, among other courses. He has coedited several books, such as *Breaking the Taboo with Young Adult Literature, Critical Explorations of Young Adult Literature: Identifying and Critiquing the Canon,* and *Critical Approaches to Teaching the High School Novel: Reinterpreting Canonical Literature.* His scholarship has been published in journals such as *Research in the Teaching of English, Teachers College Record, English Journal, Teaching and Teacher Education, The ALAN Review, Journal of Language and Literacy Education,* and *Study and Scrutiny: Research on Young Adult Literature.* Victor is the chair of the NCTE English Language Arts Educators

Commission on the Study and Teaching of Adolescent Literature and is on the board of the directors of the Assembly on Literature for Adolescents of NCTE as well as on the editorial boards of *English Journal* and *Study and Scrutiny: Research on Young Adult Literature.* Furthermore, he has appeared on *NPR* and in the *New York Times* discussing his research and teaching of the young adult novel *Speak* in relation to sexual assault and the #MeToo movement.

About the Contributors

Sarah K. Burriss is a doctoral student in the Department of Teaching and Learning at Vanderbilt University in Nashville, Tennessee. Her research focuses on digital literacies, young adult literature, and teaching and learning about ethics and advanced computational technologies, like artificial intelligence. Sarah is a former public librarian and has worked in young adult services and popular materials in Charleston, South Carolina.

Natalie Chase is a high school English teacher at Lincoln Charter School in Lincolnton, North Carolina. Natalie grew up in Massachusetts and graduated with a bachelor's degree in English studies with a concentration in secondary education from Fitchburg State University. She began her teaching career teaching high school English at Montachusett Regional Vocational Technical School and started working on her master's degree in English literature, also at Fitchburg State University. Natalie recently relocated to Charlotte, North Carolina, where she continues her passion for teaching high school English.

Anna Consalvo, PhD, is associate professor of literacy at the University of Texas at Tyler, where she teaches undergraduate and graduate courses in teacher education. After teaching middle and high school English, she earned her PhD in curriculum and instruction from UT Austin with a focus in language and literacy studies. Her research interests include youth voice and the teaching of writing, disciplinary and adolescent literacy, and aspects of young adult literature.

Katharine Covino, PhD, assistant professor of English studies, teaches writing, literature, and teacher-preparation classes at Fitchburg State University. Her research interests include critical pedagogy, gender, and identity. Her areas of current scholarship focus on (a) critical pedagogy in elementary literacy classrooms, (b) applying indigenous lenses to critically examine cultural myths, and (c) exploring disconnects that arise for novice English teachers. Additionally, she has published and presented on issues related to literacy praxis. Prior to teaching at the university level, she taught middle school and high school in Austin, Texas. She is also a children's book author, with multiple upcoming projects in the works.

Janine J. Darragh, PhD, is associate professor of literacy and ESL at the University of Idaho, where she instructs courses in English teacher preparation and young adult literature. A National Board Certified former high school English teacher of 13 years, her research interests are sociocultural and social justice issues in teaching and learning. Her current scholarship centers on supporting teachers and learners who are culturally and linguistically diverse, supporting teachers in rural poverty contexts, and trauma-sensitive teaching strategies. Her coauthored book *Reading for Action: Engaging Youth in Social Justice through Young Adult Literature* was released in 2019.

Crag Hill, a scholar of young adult literature, has published articles and chapters on young adult literature and comics and has edited a collection of essays on young adult literature, *Coming of Age: The Critical Merits of Young Adult Literature* (Routledge, 2014), and on comics, *Teaching Comics Through Multiple Lenses: Critical Perspectives* (Routledge, 2016). His latest project, coedited with Victor Malo-Juvera, is *Critical Explorations of Canonical Young Adult Literature: Identifying and Critiquing the Canon* appeared in 2020 (Routledge). They previously coedited *Critical Approaches to Teaching the High School Novel: Reinterpreting Canonical Literature* (Routledge, 2019).

Melanie Hundley, PhD, is a professor in the practice of English education at Vanderbilt University's Peabody College; her research examines how digital and multimodal composition informs the development of preservice teachers' writing pedagogy. Additionally, she explores the use of digital and social media in young adult literature. She teaches writing methods courses that focus on digital and multimodal composition and young adult literature courses that explore race, class, gender, and sexual identity in young adult texts. She has taught both middle and high school English language arts (ELA). She is currently the director of undergraduate studies for the Department of Teaching and Learning.

Kati Macaluso, PhD, is a fellow of the Institute for Educational Initiatives and an assistant professor of the Practice in the Alliance for Catholic

Education's (ACE) M.Ed. program at the University of Notre Dame. Her research focuses on English education, including ELA teacher preparation in a 21st-century context, the value of poetic literacy practices, and the spiritual and embodied dimensions of literary reading.

Michael Macaluso, PhD, is a fellow of the Institute for Educational Initiatives and an assistant professor of the practice for English ducation in the Alliance for Catholic Education at the University of Notre Dame. In addition to teaching methods and education-related courses in this role, he works with new and beginning teachers of all disciplines and grade levels—and their school systems—across the country. His primary scholarship focuses on critical approaches in English education.

Ciara Pittman, PhD, is an English teacher at Cookeville High School, where she teaches both freshmen and juniors. She has a PhD in literacy, a master's in secondary English education, and a master's in curriculum and instruction. She works as a remote learning facilitator for her school district. She serves as membership chair for the Upper Cumberland Literacy Association and supports community-based literacy initiatives.

Lisa Scherff, PhD, teaches English and AP research at the Community School of Naples. She has published more than 25 peer-reviewed articles and coauthored/coedited seven books. An award-winning educator, she received the UA College of Education's Faculty Excellence Award (2008) and the American Library Association's Intellectual Freedom Award (2008), and was selected as Lee County Schools' Secondary English Teacher of the Year (2016).

Shelly Shaffer, PhD, is an assistant professor of literacy in the Department of Education at Eastern Washington University, Cheney, Washington, where she teaches preservice elementary and secondary teachers and graduate students in education. Dr. Shaffer taught middle school and high school English for 13 years in Arizona until she earned her PhD in English education from Arizona State University in 2015. She now uses her experience, research, and education to teach courses in content area literacy and writing, secondary methods, young adult literature, children's literature, and various graduate courses. Her current research interests are young adult literature, reading motivation, flipped classrooms, mentoring, and multimedia integration in teacher education programs.

Amber Spears, PhD, is an assistant professor at Tennessee Technological University in the College of Education, where she teaches elementary methods and graduate courses in literacy. She is a former elementary school teacher and is licensed in Tennessee in K–8 elementary education, PK–3 early childhood education, and PK–12 reading specialist. She is the chair of the Upper Cumberland Literacy Association and spends her summers facilitating literacy programming for young children in her community.